THE CURIOUS CASE OF
BLACK MONEY
AND WHITE MONEY

THE CURIOUS CASE OF
BLACK MONEY
AND WHITE MONEY
EXPOSING THE DIRTY GAME OF MONEY LAUNDERING!

VARUN CHANDNA

Notion Press

Old No. 38, New No. 6
McNichols Road, Chetpet
Chennai - 600 031

First Published by Notion Press 2017
Copyright © Varun Chandna 2017
All Rights Reserved.

ISBN 978-1-946822-29-1

Dedicated to

All those who are fighting Money Laundering

in any and every way they can

In this Book, You will find 'How' all of these

$ Hawala
$ Shares and Share Market
$ Penny Stocks and Circular Trading
$ Participatory Notes (P-Notes)
$ Donations and Trusts
$ Loans and Fixed Deposits
$ Hidden Leverage
$ Convertible Financial Instruments
$ Futures and Options (F&O)
$ Bearer Shares
$ Numbered Accounts
$ Panama Islands
$ Mergers and Acquisitions (M&A)
$ Real Estate
$ Letters of Credit (L/C)
$ International Trade (Import & Export)
$ Special Economic Zones (SEZ/ Free Trade Zones (FTZ))
$ Gold
$ Diamonds
$ Bitcoins
$ Gambling
$ Start-ups etc.

...may be related with Money Laundering

Contents

Contents

Preface

"I'm tired of dreaming. I'm into doing at the moment."

— Bono
(Irish Singer and Writer)

While I was preparing for my Chartered Accountancy Exams in early 2000s, some of my friends and relatives used to tell me that the main business of a Chartered Accountant (CA) is to manage the money of his High Net worth clients and convert their black money (Dirty Money or No. 2 money) into white (Clean Money or No. 1 Money). I had no real idea of this business and had doubts over their knowledge on black and white money too but their comments gave me an innocent kind of a proud feeling that like a pilot flies an aeroplane so intelligently pushing a lot of buttons up and down, I too would be doing some complex and sophisticated kind of a job.

However, in my entire CA curriculum, there was no subject that would teach me about this intricate job. After completing my CA, I went into the financial and banking sector jobs where trainings on legal compliances and Anti-Money Laundering were a regular affair but still they never focussed on how the launderers actually worked. While working with Bank of Tokyo-Mitsubishi UFJ, I used to think about generation and laundering of black money being a big menace to our country and a lot of statistics also suggested the size of this shadow economy to be no lesser than the real economy.

This made me even more interested in this topic and I decided to look out for the modus operandi that worked behind the scene in conversion of black money into white money and bring them out in public glare so that everybody understands it and there is nothing that is known only to launderers, government and a few professionals.

Knowing the ways in which money launderers abuse laws will also help people in understanding the complexity of these schemes which government agencies deal with and at the same time appreciate the steps government is taking in this direction.

As I studied the topic with greater interest, I thought of putting in some sincere efforts to help my fellow countrymen and people around this world tackle this menace of black money by spreading awareness and thought of coming out with a book on this topic. I believe if criminals fear that no matter how successful they are at the crime itself, there will still be problems in disposing off the loot, crime rate will definitely fall.

There are various people from different facets of society – professionals as well as students who want to know 'how' exactly the game of black to white is played. They may or may not be financial experts or finance enthusiasts but anyone who is interested in financial and economic activities should find this book useful.

Revenue and tax officials across the world would most likely be aware of most of the methods discussed here but a revisit to the basics is always beneficial and if they can effectively address all that, what is written here, Money Laundering is sure to get a big blow.

When I moved towards this subject in Feb' 2016, there was a buzz around this black money word but there wasn't much that was done to prevent money laundering. However, things have changed significantly since then. Government of India has taken various measures to curb black money and money laundering. It had enacted a draconian Black Money Law in 2015 and then came out with an Income Disclosure Scheme in 2016 whereby it gave a window to black money holders to disclose their black money or else face prosecution.

Continuing the series, it demonetised high value currency notes of INR 500 and INR 1000 in 2016, extended the tax amnesty schemes and then legislated various Anti-Abuse measures in Union Budget of 2017 which shall become law effective from 01st April, 2017. It has since revised Tax Treaties with few Tax Haven countries also.

The above measures are not all; the Government is stead-fast on this issue of Black Money and is working on various facets related to it, be it *Benami* (Anonymous) Transaction Law, revisions in Income Tax Law, enacting Goods & Service Tax (GST) Law to replace existing Indirect Tax Laws, revisions in Corporate Law, Securities Law etc. Going through the methods stated in this book, readers will be able to evaluate the complexity embedded in the schemes and the changes made in various laws with respect to them.

Many of the measures taken by the government have already curbed and/or killed certain methods mentioned in this book while others may become redundant due to future legislations coming from government but they shall always be present here and relevant for academic purposes. I believe that besides garnering interest of various professionals like CAs, CSs, CMAs, MBAs and the students pursuing these courses, this book shall be relevant for bankers especially Credit Analysts, Relationship Managers and Trade Finance officials; Stock Brokers, Revenue Officials as well as public at large who is in anyways interested in Black Money and White Money.

Getting into the book: Few requests please

Please note that all the Money Laundering transactions are complex because if they are not devised that way, they would be easily identified. The Money Laundering game played between government and money launderers is like Tom and Jerry contest where whoever can think from other's perspective will most likely win and therefore it's marred with complexity and shrewdness. However, I have tried to keep it simple so that the idea easily creeps into everybody's mind. The amounts used are also small for understanding purposes. I have generally used INR 1 Million (or Mio) in most of my examples and INR 1 when read as USD 1 automatically becomes 70 times higher.

I humbly request the readers to read through all sections and pages sequentially – page by page from the very first page to the last one to have a better understanding of the subject as well as author's perspective. After all, it's just 200 pages of real content that is presented before you.

Try to keep a pen and paper with you while analysing the figures stated in some of the methods.

Though every care has been taken to avoid mistakes, yet it is futile to expect no mistake due to a lot of legality and figures involved. Further, the room of improvement is always there. Therefore I shall be obliged to receive all sorts of comments, suggestions and criticisms from my readers. My e-mail id is: varun.chandna@hotmail.com

Disclaimers and Representations:

This book – *The Curious Case of Black Money and White Money... Exposing the dirty game of Money Laundering!* has been written to bring into public limelight the ways and tools commonly used by crooks to convert their illegitimate (black) money to legitimate (white) money. Although the book has been written from an Indian perspective but readers across boundaries shall find it useful.

The methods stated here are only for academic interests and for no other purpose.

I have personally neither used any of the methods or modus operandi stated herein nor met with any person who uses them.

Experts would understand that Government of India has stipulated various measures in the International Taxation arena like General Anti-Avoidance Measures (GAAR), rules on Place of Effective Management (POEM) and Base Erosion in Profit Shifting (BEPS), Auto-Exchange of Tax Information between countries, Amendments in Tax Treaties with Tax Havens and many more; all of which give precedence to substance over form and are aimed at tax avoidance and money laundering through abuse of various loopholes. Government of today has the power to disregard any structure, any modus-operandi that has been created to avoid tax and/or smells of money laundering. It has powers vide enough within Taxation law, Foreign Exchange Law, Benami Property Law and Black Money Law to confiscate all the Dirty Money of a person. I salute the government for its efforts.

This book is not subject to any expert opinion and is aimed at presenting an interesting and valuable content to its readers.

The book does not contain any amount of expert advice on any of the schemes listed herein. All the modus operandi and methods stated here are as result of in-depth research on the subject intended to benefit investigators and douse curiosity of people interested in knowing the 'how' of Money Laundering. The book neither contains any professional advice nor is a substitute for any professional or expert advice with respect to its subject.

My intention of writing this book is to explain Money Laundering to everyone in an interesting manner. For this purpose, I have used examples of some common malpractices that facilitate conversion of Black Money into White. This would also enable various readers to understand the rationale behind barrage of anti-abuse measures introduced by government in a better way and delve into their details, if and when required since none of the methods of laundering money is unknown to the government.

The characters and names used in this book are fictitious. Any resemblance to actual persons, living or dead, or actual events is purely unintentional.

It is a coincidence that as I was writing this book to expose ways of laundering money, Government of India decided to demonetise INR 500 and INR 1000 currency notes. While demonetisation is definitely a positive step towards curbing the menace of black money but it targets only one way of storing black money – cash and does little to stop further generation and laundering of black money. However, I understand that government is taking many more steps in conjunction to demonetisation and gradually making it more and more difficult to launder black money with each passing day.

I believe that black money is always bad for the world and majority of its population as it increases the disparity between the rich and the poor.

At last I would like to state that that we in India worship Goddess *Laxmi* as Goddess of Wealth and use a phrase *"Subh Labh"* which means auspicious (Subh) Profit (Labh). This implies that we should definitely aspire for wealth and profit but it should be auspicious and pure. It should not be dirty or black. It should come from legitimate sources and after payment of due taxes. Then only Goddess will be happy and bestow her blessings upon us.

With this message, let us embark upon this journey of uncovering the strategies used by many rich and immoral towards changing the colour of their money from black to white passing through the moves made by government in this respect.

I hope you enjoy the read!!

– Varun Chandna
09th February, 2017

Acknowledgements

When I sit back and think of people who contributed immensely towards making this book a reality, a long list of names comes to my mind.

The first name that comes up is Mr Rajiv Kumar Mahajan who is not just my father-in-law but also a seasoned Chartered Accountant with around 30 years of professional experience. I thank him for all the invaluable inputs he gave in this book, which would have remained incomplete without him.

I thank Mother o' Mine, Mrs Sunita Chandna as I believe that anything I do well in my life is because of her.

I thank my father – Mr Harish Chandna and my mother-in-law – Mrs Sunita Mahajan for continuously showering their blessings upon me.

I thank my wife Shradha who stood like a wall of support behind me while I tried to become an author.

I thank my four-year-old son Dhavit, whose mischiefs and small stories kept my mind laundered from boredom throughout this endeavour of mine.

I thank my mamaji and mamiji – Mr Ramesh Thapar and Mrs Ranjana Thapar who were equally excited about this book and provided valuable suggestions to make it a success.

I thank Ms. Esha R. Garg for providing me with all the images used in this book in perfect time.

I am thankful to Mr K Subramanian of NumeroUno Academy and Mr Praloy Majumder of Disseminare Consulting for their training programmes on Anti-Money Laundering.

I am also thankful to all my readers for reposing confidence in me by deciding to buy this book.

And last but not the least I thank Ms Yamini Shekar, Ms. Thaatcher Missier and the entire team of Notion Press that worked very hard to publish this book at the earliest.

Thank you and God bless you all.

The Great Demonetisation of India and the Check Mate Moves Played by Both Sides

As stated in my preface that Demonetisation of High Denomination Currency notes happened in India at the same time when I was preparing this book. It is undoubtedly a nice coincidence and since this whole exercise is related to curbing of black money, it becomes imperative for me to mention about this bold move of government as well as its loop holes that got exploited.

Demonetisation of currency notes is one step that is sure to find its place whenever suggestions are drafted by political think tanks on how to curb the black money or shadow economy.

Government of India (GoI) too, relying upon the power of demonetisation to curb the menace of black money, demonetised its highest value currency notes of INR 500 and INR 1000 w.e.f. 09-Nov-2016 and gave a window of 51 days to everyone to exchange/convert the demonetised currency notes into new notes through banks till 30-Dec-2016 (31st December being a bank holiday). It also launched a new version of INR 500 currency note and an altogether new denomination of INR 2000 currency note at the same time.

Government thought that since currency notes of these two denominations together accounted for approximately 86% of the total currency in circulation in India, banning them would hit black money hoarders the hardest. The intentions might be correct but what happened in its aftermath was completely unexpected. People devised several innovative but illegitimate ways to convert their demonetised currency into valid currency. There was cash crunch in the whole country as the banks did not had adequate cash to meet everyone's demands, ATMs remained dry most of the time, the new 2000 currency note did not fit the specifications of these machines, there were unending queues of people waiting outside banks and ATMs for hours, there were deaths, there were layoffs, political back lash, non-functioning of parliament, what all and what not.

Even though there were benefits that were to accrue in the medium to long term, there were seizures of unaccounted money of INR 30 to 40 Billion but the costs of demonetisation cannot be ignored. Profits were lost, jobs were lost, economic growth was lost and even lives were lost.

Moreover, it should be noted that cash is just one of the means of holding black money. Other prominent means through which black money is held are as follows:

$ Bank Accounts (On-shore) either in own name, business/front company's name or in the name of some trusted lieutenants.

$ Bank Accounts (offshore through offshore shell corporations in the manner stated above)

$ Shares and other securities in a business either in own name, business/ front company's name or in the name of some trusted lieutenants.

$ Gold, Diamonds and other precious stones

$ Real Estate

$ Luxury Items like Cars, Watches etc.

$ Assets of Bogus Business/Front Companies etc.

Therefore Government of any country targeting black money needs to target all the above means and not just cash. GoI is understandably targeting all of them systematically but then going after all the aforementioned means will only target the existing hoards of black money. What about the hoards getting piled up today and tomorrow post demonetisation. Thus, it is the generation of black money that needs to be targeted.

No country can afford to ignore the ingenuity of people when it comes to money. Since this whole book is about such clever activities, I would rather focus on them in this chapter.

In the wake of demonetisation, there were various ingenuous ways in which Indian people exchanged their demonetised cash. Some interesting ones are stated here:

Gold and Jewellery:

As soon as the demonetisation announcement was made around 8 pm on 08-Nov-2016, jewellers of all sorts witnessed unprecedented sales of their accounted and unaccounted stock.

Around 8 pm, Prime Minister announced that High Value Currency Notes of INR 500 and INR 1000 will cease to be a legal tender from 12 pm (midnight) and black money holders went on a buying spree to make the maximum use of these 4 hours. They decided to buy gold, diamonds and jewellery with it and the gold rate, pegged to international rate which was trading around INR 28,000 per 10 grams before this announcement shot up to INR 50,000 per gram in a single night. This unofficial rally lasted for few days as jewellers made back dated sales in their accounts, under-invoiced their sales or even skipped that if their stock was unaccounted.

Soon after, the Government went after many such jewellers through its search and seizure procedures which eventually curbed this malpractice to a large extent.

Cooperative Banks:

Cooperative Banks are mainly located in the rural areas and most of these are not computerized. Hence several banking operations take place manually.

Soon after the announcement of demonetisation, many people holding unaccounted cash in form of the demonetised High Value Notes (HVN) of INR 500 and INR 1000 deposited them in these banks in back value dated transactions and also opened back dated Fixed Deposit accounts taking advantage of manual entries and lax procedures.

Another way devised was issuance of demand drafts and pay orders against old notes. According to reports, the deal between the cooperative banks and the persons buying the demand draft was that they will not present these instruments to any other banks for encashment and after 31st March (end of Financial Year), the issuing cooperative banks will cancel these instruments and return money to the holders in new currency notes. This will not leave any significant trail as it will be cash exchanged against cash.

As soon as the government got a cue of all this, it stopped cooperative banks from accepting old notes for deposit or exchange.

Use of poor as middlemen:

The idea behind demonetisation was to curb black money hoarded by rich people and undoubtedly these people were ought to be big businessmen, politicians, bureaucrats, celebrities etc. but none of these people were found standing in queues in front of banks for exchanging their old notes into new.

It was only poor and middle class people who were waiting outside the bank to get currency exchanged. However, whose currency was it, remains a question.

The rich and influential had other ways of exchanging currency, some known and some unknown not fit to be commented upon. They hired poor to get the job done who stood outside banks day in and day out, in multiples for several days earning a regular commission. Many identification proofs of unrelated people including own employees was misused for the purpose of exchanging demonetised notes for valid ones.

The government responded through various regulations and thresholds that restricted exchange, deposits and withdrawals from bank accounts. Banks used indelible ink on the fingers of people suspected to be doing rounds.

Deposit though Jan Dhan Accounts (Small Savings Bank Accounts):

Government of India through a scheme - Pradhan Mantri Jan Dhan Yojana (PMJDY) had opened around 240 million bank accounts of the poor people with a view of implementing financial inclusion and providing basic banking facility to the poor. Jan Dhan Bank Account holders are not required to comply with Know Your Customer (KYC) norms in the first year of operation. The idea was to ensure that every citizen of the country gets a bank account without any hassles. However, within a couple of weeks from the demonetisation announcement, it was seen that abnormally huge amounts of the discontinued HVN are being deposited in the Jan Dhan Accounts.

Hoarders of unaccounted cash used the accounts of the poor to deposit their black money. They handed a certain sum of money to the original account holder and convinced him to deposit such amount in the account. The account holder was required to withdraw the money in small amounts and pay it back to the black money holder from time to time in new notes.

The government however clarified that it will tax and seize any unaccounted money found deposited in such a manner. But does it have the resources to do so is a mystery. Secondly, it is difficult to identify and trace these account holders for the want of KYC procedures. They might even disclose small incomes and savings to prove their deposits.

Temples and Charitable Trusts:

India is known for its temples and religiousness. Post demonetisation, there was a surge in giving donations through the discontinued 500 and 1000 notes.

Temples and Trusts keep getting huge amounts of donations from people and generally these are in currency lower than 500 and 1000. Therefore, as per media reports, some temples and trusts accepted the demonetised notes from the black money holders and paid them back in lower denomination notes after deducting a commission.

Petrol Pumps:

Petrol Pumps were allowed to accept old notes up to a certain period of time so that people do not face any inconvenience. This advantage provided by the government was misused by many black money holders who exchanged their old notes for new notes by giving them a commission.

Toll Plazas:

Like petrol pumps, toll plazas on national highways too have large amounts of smaller denomination currency. It was likewise misused for conversion. However, government soon relaxed toll tax collection on national highways.

Theatres:

Many theatres accept advance cash bookings for their tickets. They invariably have an excuse to exchange old cash with new one. Subsequently, the show gets cancelled and the money is returned after deduction of a commission.

Train Tickets:

Keeping in mind, the inconvenience to be faced by people as a result of demonetisation, the government allowed the use of discontinued 500 rupee and 1000 rupee notes for the purpose of buying train tickets till certain period of time. Several black money holders took this opportunity to convert some of their black money into white. It's no small game, more than twenty million people travel through Indian railways every day.

Soon after demonetisation came into effect, there was a huge surge in the number of train tickets bought. The idea was to buy as many train tickets as possible across the reservation counter and cancel these tickets later on. The railways are supposed to charge a nominal cancellation fee and return the rest of the money in cash in form of valid notes. However the government quickly read the intention and announced that ticket cancellation refunds will be credited to bank accounts instead of paying in cash.

Money Changers:

Several money changers emerged all across the country. With the view of earning some quick profit by taking advantage of the demonetisation move, these people offered exchange of old discontinued notes for smaller denomination notes or new notes for a commission ranging from 20% to 50%. They also sold US Dollars and other currencies physically in return for the demonetised notes for a hefty commission.

Banks:

There were reports claiming the involvement of many bank employees as well as officials from Reserve Bank of India (RBI) helping the black money holders convert their demonetised money into new currency notes.

Political Parties:

Since Political Parties in India are exempt from Income Tax on their income, deposit of cash in their bank accounts even though in demonetised notes would not attract any tax and thus many parties exploited this privilege to convert demonetised currency notes into legally valid ones.

Election Campaigning:

Nothing is hidden about political parties receiving large amounts of donations in cash. A major portion of this cash is used in campaigning before elections.

Post demonetisation, by-elections were held in certain states, where the political parties used this method to convert their black money. In some places, the political parties reportedly distributed cash to a significant number of voters to gain their votes. Some voters were also given interest free loan with the condition of returning the amount after a year, in new notes. Assenting voters got commission.

Demonetisation Facts:

In response to a Right to Information (RTI) application, Reserve Bank of India (RBI) informed that on 08th November, 2016 – the date on which demonetisation was announced, there were INR 20.51 Trillion worth of INR 500 and INR 1000 currency notes in India and adjusting it for stock of such notes held with RBI/Banks, the demonetised notes in circulation, were approximately INR 15.45 Trillion.

No official figures on value of demonetised notes deposited in banks till 30-Dec-2016 (last date for old currency exchange at banks) have been released by RBI yet (as of 09-Feb-2017) but data in public domain suggests the figure is close to INR 14.97 Trillion which is ~97% of the amount in circulation when the move was announced.

Adjusting the deposit figure for notes held by Non Resident Indians (NRIs), residents travelling abroad during the demonetisation period as well as other residents who can still deposit them with RBI directly by giving proper declarations, it can be said that demonetisation failed in deterring people from depositing their unaccounted cash into the banking system. However it should be noted that the unaccounted cash so deposited does not become white/ legitimate just because it entered the banking system.

Although there are no reliable estimates of black money generation or accumulation in India and also there is no well accepted method for making such estimation but still the black money / shadow economy of India has been estimated anywhere from 20% to 30% of its GDP by various sources over a period of time. World Bank Development Research Group estimated the shadow economies of 162 countries from 1999 to 2007. It reported that the weighted average size of the shadow economy as a percentage of official GDP of these 162 countries in 2007 was 31%. For India, this figure was 23.2%. (Source: White Paper on black money, May 2012 released by Ministry of Finance, GoI). Similarly, Bank of America Merrill Lynch (BoAML) estimated India's Black Economy at 25% to 30% of its GDP. With Indian GDP at USD 2.30 Trillion, the 25% figure comes to INR 38 Trillion, much larger than the entire cash in circulation; forget about just high value notes. Accordingly, as I stated in the beginning of this chapter, there are many forms in which black money is held, stored and transmitted, cash being just one of them. But all said and done, demonetisation was an audacious move of our prime minister – Mr Narendra Modi who made his intentions clear on black money and proved that he can go to any extent on curbing this menace. Though it is for the experts to decide whether his move was really cost effective in unearthing black money or not but his decision has definitely provided three major benefits:

1. Counterfeit Currency got blown off to the maximum extent possible.
2. Terrorist Financing got a severe hit.
3. India got a digital boost which will increase transparency as well as knowledge and awareness of people towards digitization going forward.

Moreover, if cash in circulation is reduced, there will be higher transparency, higher tax base and lower black money. Not to forget that government of India is acting on all fronts to reduce black money be it cash or otherwise.

Union Budget 2017: Directions Towards Clean India — Directions Towards Clean Money

In India, presentation of Financial Budget by Central Government is an exciting Annual Event which generally takes place in the month of February and is looked upon by many professionals for knowing how the changes proposed in the budget will affect the accounting, profitability and taxation aspects of their businesses or that of their clients.

These changes as proposed in February every year are generally applicable from the upcoming Financial Year that begins on 1st April and ends after 12 months on 31st March.

The Union Budget or say Finance Bill of 2017 presented on 1st February, 2017 was special for various reasons:

- ✓ *It came right after the historic move of demonetisation of high value currency notes by Government.*
- ✓ *The Budget gave a direction and clarity over government's thinking that it is extremely serious on curbing the menace of black money.*
- ✓ *It incorporated Railway Budget too which was being presented separately for the past 92 years.*

Various significant measures were introduced by the Government of India. Some of them, relevant for the purposes of this book are briefly stated here:

The Finance Bill of 2017 has broadly and subject to fine details:

- ✓ Promoted Digital Economy by curbing the use of cash in various ways and giving tax incentives with respect to non-cash turnover of small and medium tax payers.
- ✓ Reduced the maximum amount of cash expenditure allowable under the Income Tax Act from INR 20,000 to INR 10,000.

- ✓ Prohibited all transactions in cash above INR 300,000 unless the reason holds sufficient merit.

- ✓ Reduced the limit of cash donation which can be received by a charitable trust from INR 10,000 to INR 2,000.

- ✓ Induced the much needed electoral reforms by reducing the maximum amount of cash donation that a political party can receive to INR 2,000 from INR 20,000.

- ✓ Initiated political reforms by proposing amendment to Reserve Bank of India (RBI) Act to issue electoral bonds which shall be purchased through banking channels by the donor and redeemed in the bank account of political party of his choice.

- ✓ Reduced the time limit from 3 years to 2 years for an immovable property to be classified as Long Term with respect to capital gain or loss giving much needed fillip to the Real Estate sector. Similarly, the time limit has reduced for unlisted shares also from 3 years to 2 years.

- ✓ Previously, income from sale of long term listed shares (i.e. those held for at least 1 year) was exempt even if the purchase of such shares was not through stock exchanges. Now, they will be taxable if Securities Transaction Tax (tax charged when traded on stock exchange) was not charged when they were purchased. This is aimed to curb the use of physical shares in money laundering.

- ✓ Provided that where the sale amount of shares (other than listed shares) is less than the Fair Market Value (FMV), the FMV will be taken as sale amount for capital gains taxation.

- ✓ Previously, gifts (i.e. transfer of money or any movable or immovable property for free or inadequate consideration) in excess of INR 50,000 in a financial year were taxable only in hands of Individuals, Hindu Undivided Families (HUFs), Companies and Firms while it was not taxable in the hands of certain trusts and institutions. Now no entity including trusts and institutions is exempt and it will have to shell out tax on receipt of gifts.

- ✓ Provided that Interest Expense claimed by an entity as paid to its associated entity for loan received from it shall be restricted to 30% of payer's EBITDA (Earnings Before Interest Tax Depreciation and Amortisation).

- ✓ Provided for mandatory filing of Income Tax Return by various Income Tax Exempt entities and increased the fee for delayed filing of Income Tax Returns by all persons.

✓ Imposed penalties on various professionals including chartered accountants for furnishing of incorrect information in their reports and/or certificates.

✓ Provided more teeth to the tax department by providing that the reasons recorded by the department for conducting a search and/or seizure referred to as 'reasons to believe' or 'reasons to suspect' shall not be disclosed to any person or any authority lower than Courts including Appellate Tribunal.

By undertaking the above measures, the government has tried to curb the use of black money and various ways of laundering black money. We will refer to the related provisions of this Budget while we go through the methods specified herein. Let us now start.

Introduction to the Book

"It's bad form to mention Money Laundering. Instead you talk about asset management structures and tax beneficial schemes"

–John Sweeney
(Noted Journalist)

No Book on Money Laundering can start or complete without answering some basic questions. They are:

What is Money Laundering?

Money laundering simply means conversion of black money (Dirty Money) into white money (Clean Money) where the black money may not become white legally but appear to have become so.

The process of Money Laundering is also known as Jama Kharchi in India.

Although the aforementioned definition looks pretty simple but three questions emanate at once from the said statement:

1. What is black money?
2. What is white money?
3. Why is conversion of black money into white money required?

The explanations are as follows:

Black Money (or Dirty Money):

If someone is concealing his actual money, he is not just concealing that money but also the crime behind that. The crime can be either evasion of taxes or more than that.

If I have got some money and I cannot legally and publicly disclose and elaborate its source, it implies this is my black money.

This money may come from any illegal activity which I cannot disclose to have carried out or may be still carrying out. Examples include Drug Trade, Flesh Trade,

Poaching of Animals, Arms Trade, Contract Killing, Theft, Prostitution, Bootlegging (like selling alcohol and other prohibited items illegally), taking of bribes, receiving kickbacks, Illegal Mining, Illegal Trade, fraudulently undertaking a business without its permit/license either wholly or partly or any other illegal activity of any sort.

Dirty money also includes money coming from absolutely legal activities but not disclosed to government in an attempt to save or say evade taxes.

Had there been no taxes, there would have been no black money of this sort. The idea that government wants a slice of whatever you earn leads to concealment even if the tax rate is 1%. In reality though it is many times higher than this 1% and there is an added cost of compliance. Taxes may undoubtedly be necessary but have created liars out of people.

Even if the business and activities are legal but full income and actual expenses there from is not disclosed to government authorities to avoid paying taxes on them, it amounts to black money. This concealment is done by businesses by maintaining two sets of accounts; one to be disclosed to the government and other to be kept for the actual holistic view of business.

White Money (or Clean Money):

If I have got some money and I can legally and publicly announce the source of my money, it implies this is my white money.

This money comes from a completely legal, compliant and transparent source. If I disclosed all my income and its source completely to the government and paid all applicable taxes on the same, there is no fear of being questioned about it.

Conversion of black money (Dirty Money) into white money (Clean Money): Money Laundering

Conversion of black money into white money is the method or process by which Dirty Money appears to be clean.

Due to various rules, regulations and legislations; spending of black money is sometimes more difficult than earning it and this is not a new phenomenon:

Long back in late 18th century, there used to be some sea pirates who had their piracy business spanning across Indian and Atlantic Oceans. They were successful in amassing huge wealth by looting the ships that would come their way. After accumulating heavy sums of money, jewellery and valuable commodities, they decided to settle in England but their spending profligacy soon drew the civilised attention towards them and they got arrested.

Then some 100 years later in 1931 in Chicago; Alphonse Capone who was involved in all sorts of crime, be it boot legging, prostitution, bribery, treason, gambling etc. was sentenced to eleven years in federal prison not because of his underworld activities but for non-payment of due taxes on money garnered from of such activities when the crimes undertaken by him could not be proved for the want of evidence and adequate legislation.

Since then the government authorities have got their principle right that if they cannot book the tainted person directly, they should go after his tainted money.

Keeping black money is always dangerous as governments around the world are stressing on its forfeiture as and when detected. Besides forfeiture, there can be penalties for concealment of income which would be over and above the amount forfeited. Secondly, this will take a toll on the criminal personally as investigation against him will strengthen and he will land in prison.

Money launderers of today understand that even though it may be easy to earn the black money, it is not that easy to dispose of the money so accumulated. Accumulating black money will serve any purpose only when it can be utilized to buy the luxuries and worldly pleasures which its value commands.

They know that everything bad could happen to them, if their loot is traced back to them and therefore they use various methods to disguise the colour or source of their black money.

Therefore, for the purpose of its spending and disposition, the black money should appear clean and from legitimate source so that it is not questioned or investigated or even if investigated, it is not caught since it has become clean/ white through the process of Money Laundering.

This book makes an attempt to lucidly explain to the general public and lay man like me, the methods, techniques and schemes that are used in Money Laundering.

Stages in Money Laundering

Before proceeding with the methods, let me explain that all the Money Laundering schemes pass through following three stages:

1. **Placement Stage:** This is the 1st stage of a Money Laundering Scheme. Here the form of the money is changed or converted from physical to non-physical. Since large purchases in simply cash attract suspicion, they need to be channelized into bank accounts. For example, Mr Darkhorse who has loads of black money in form of cash starts depositing small sums in his bank accounts regularly in one way or the other.

   The positive side of placement for Mr Darkhorse is that now he has channelized his money in bank account from which he can easily utilize the funds without attracting much of suspicion.

The negative side of placement for Mr Darkhorse however is that since the money is placed in bank accounts, all the transactions will get reflected in the account statements leaving a documentary paper trail.

2. **Layering Stage:** This stage is used to weed out the negative side of the placement stage by disguising the transaction through various means including making it more complex and complicated. For example, Mr Jockey, an agent hired by Mr Darkhorse does not deposit the money into Mr Whitehorse's account directly but instead into the accounts of his affiliates or that of a farce business company and circulates it back and forth a number of times before the money ultimately reaches Darkhorse's bank account or comes to his disposal. This circulation of money may even include different countries so as to disrupt the investigation of paper trail.

3. **Integration Stage:** This is the final stage whereby the black money holder finds some justification for explaining the source of his white money converted from his black money. In this stage therefore, Mr Darkhorse demonstrates that the Money Laundering transaction was authentic and the money has come from his genuine business. He pretends to be a successful businessman earning much more than his business is actually worth (bogus business company) or he shows the funds as unsecured loan (bogus loan entry) in his bank account from another person etc.

The knowledge of the aforementioned stages help in decoding a Money Laundering transaction. For example, if it is revealed that Mr Darkhorse has been successful in placing money into his bank accounts, the investigating officer gets prepared for peeling off the layering transactions carried out subsequently.

Black Money always remains Black

People often confuse that Money Laundering is a process that successfully converts black money into white which is wrong. It is actually the appearance that changes form. After Money Laundering process is applied, it rinses or paints the black money so that it appears white but that money will never get off its original black colour. Once a black money, always the black money goes the rule. Thus deposit of unaccounted cash in bank account due to demonetisation does not make it white.

For example: If Mr Darkhorse has earned black money from flesh trade and prostitution but is successful to show it as his business or Capital Gain, it will only appear as white but not become white. Investigators, *on finding evidence* of the crime are always free to apply legal provisions on such income. Any asset, expenditure or investment made through black money is also black. It has just changed form.

But yes, there exists a fool proof way of converting black money into white and ironically that is provided by governments themselves in form of Voluntary Disclosure or Tax Amnesty Schemes whereby the government, after levying a tax and penalty on the voluntarily declared black money, guarantees not to question its source of income.

Ill-effects of Money Laundering

Ill-effects of Money Laundering are two-fold:

$ **It encourages Disparity of income:** The rich becomes richer and the poor becomes poorer. Since the rich indulge in undisclosed malpractices, they accumulate wealth that is illegitimate whereas the unprivileged bear the maximum brunt of corruption, inflation, unfair competition, lack of basic amenities like education, health, electricity etc.

$ **It encourages Crime:** If it is easy to disguise black money into white through Money Laundering, it encourages all activities that generate black money and therefore facilitates the ill-effects of all such crimes.

Regulatory Framework:

Governments across the world are striving to curb the menace of black money and money laundering. There are thresholds of cash deposits in banks beyond which identification proofs are required to be furnished by banks. In India, Permanent Account Number (Income Tax Identification Number) is required if amount of cash deposit is INR 50,000 or more in a single transaction. In USA, I think this limit is USD 10,000 and likewise in other countries. Then banks need to file Cash Transaction Reports (CTR) with Financial Intelligence Unit (FIU) of respective countries if annual deposits in cash into a bank account in aggregate exceed a threshold amount say INR 1 Million. Besides CTR a Suspicious Transaction Report (STR) needs to be filed by banks whenever they find a transaction to be suspicious with respect to Money Laundering. All such CTR and STR transactions are then investigated thoroughly by FIU. FIU collects similar data from various organisations and investigates the matter.

In India, we have Prevention of Money Laundering Act (PMLA), 2002 and Black Money (Undisclosed Foreign Income and Assets) and Imposition of Tax Act, 2015 as well as a dedicated department in form of Enforcement Directorate to deal with Money Laundering crimes. Besides this, provisions of Income Tax Act 1961 and Companies Act 2013 are refined time and again to curb any misuse for Money Laundering. The changes proposed in Income Tax Act by Finance Bill 2017 contain various provisions with respect to curbing the menace of black money as discussed in the previous chapter.

Government is going ahead with various measures like enforcement of Benami *(meaning anonymous)* Properties (Prohibition) Amendment Act 2016. Many Penny Stocks have already been compulsorily de-listed by the stock exchanges. Goods and Service Tax (GST) will soon be a reality in India which will further curb many malpractices prevalent in businesses through transparency.

On international front, GoI is revising its Double Tax Avoidance Agreements (DTAA) / Tax Treaties with various tax havens which will reduce the tax advantage available from these countries and also encourage efficient information exchange about Indians holding companies and bank accounts in such countries. Tax Treaties with Mauritius and Cyprus have already been revised.

Banks across the world including India are getting strict on Money Laundering. Hefty fines have been imposed on many big banks for non-compliance with respect to laxity in KYC and Anti-Money Laundering procedures. In advanced countries, some Foreign Banks have even lost banking licenses due to the same. In India, RBI is stressing hard on rigorous verification of KYC data and due diligence of its customers and may soon start penalising immensely for non-compliance of Anti-Money Laundering (AML) procedures.

FATF (Financial Action Task Force) which is an international organisation with a global network to combat Money Laundering is also working hard to make international and trade based money laundering as difficult as possible. It has 37 member countries and more than 190 jurisdictions that have committed to its recommendations.

All of this is not exhaustive and new means are continuously being promulgated to curb black money and money laundering.

Characters in the book:

For explanation purposes, I have used three characters in this book:

1. **Mr Darkhorse**: He is the real crook. He has got all the black money accumulated from one and many illicit activities.
2. **Mr Whitehorse**: He is a businessman and not a criminal as such, but by colluding with Darkhorse to support his business, becomes one.
3. **Mr Jockey**: He is the intermediary between Mr Darkhorse and Mr Whitehorse and due to his knowledge, connections and nexus with other people like him, Darkhorse and Whitehorse, he is the agent and the think tank in a Money Laundering transaction.

(Mr Darkhorse)

Mr Darkhorse has accumulated huge amounts of black money through illegal activities like:

$ Narcotics and/or Illegal drug trade (smuggling of opium, marijuana etc.)

$ Extortion, bootlegging, murders and other crimes

$ Betting on cricket, football games etc. which is illegal.

$ Import of various goods into the country without payment of required customs duty.

$ Undertaking prohibited trades.

$ Corruption (Receiving of bribes), Non-Disclosure of actual income.

$ Non-Payment of due taxes.

(Mr Whitehorse)

Mr. Whitehorse is a businessman who is concerned only with his business interests. However, the system requires him to please various authorities who are generally not pleased by the growth of his business but by what his business has got to offer them and so he also enters this game.

He may also get lured by his selfish interest to save money by evading taxes.

Further he may be one of those who are willing to join this game for personal, professional gains like commissions coming his way.

Whitehorse generally plays the role of counterparty to Mr Darkhorse.

Mr Jockey is the real expert of this Money Laundering game. He is like a director of a movie who has been hired by the above characters to fulfil their malicious intentions.

Jockey can be an accountant, an attorney, a Hawala operator etc. who specialises in the techniques and methods of Money Laundering.

Since, Mr Darkhorse and Mr Whitehorse generally do not know each other because of their different businesses; it is Mr Jockey's job to facilitate the purposes of both of them.

He plays a counterparty to Mr Darkhorse or to Mr Whitehorse or to both.

(Mr Jockey)

The real objective behind Money Laundering scheme is that the black money holder wants to enjoy his ill-gotten money without any fear of getting caught by tax officials, who can forfeit his entire black money.

For example: Mr Darkhorse is a successful businessman who has accumulated hoards of unaccounted money - black money by underreporting the income of his tobacco and dairy farm business i.e. if he made sales of INR 1000, he showed only INR 600 to tax authorities, remaining INR 400 was not recorded officially but in parallel books of accounts. Even in the INR 600 sales shown to tax authorities, the sales amount was adjusted for many expenses that were fictitious / inflated. By doing so over years, he has accumulated huge amounts of (black) money that is not reported to government.

Darkhorse could also be a corrupt government official who misuses the powers of his office to garner huge amount of black income through bribes.

The point here is that Darkhorse has much more money than that declared and he does not want to lose that to tax investigation and confiscation. Moreover, he is also afraid of the damage to his reputation and questions which may be asked about the source of his black money.

It may be even so that he wants to buy a bungalow or a luxury car, price of which is higher than his corpus in white (books of accounts) and therefore the purchase requires him to convert some of his black money into white.

In all such case therefore, Darkhorse badly needs a Money Laundering scheme to help convert his black money into white.

Ways to Transfer Money and Hawala

There is always more than one way to remit money.

The Authentic Way: Wire Transfer

When Samuel Morse developed Electrical Telegraph in 1937 and sent first telegraphic message in 1938 covering a distance of just three kilometres, no one would have imagined that this method of transferring message will one day be used to handle all the money transfers in this world.

Now trillions of dollars move every single day globally on the strength of few electronic signals.

Electronic Funds Transfer (EFT) as they call it is a method of transferring money from one bank account to another. There are three major EFT systems in the world:

1. **SWIFT** (Society for Worldwide Interbank Financial Telecommunication) is an international network which enables Banks/ Financial Institutions to send and receive information about financial transactions in a secure and standardized environment. Majority of interbank messages use SWIFT Network for facilitating international payments.

2. **Fedwire** (Federal Reserve Wire Network) is the primary U.S. network used for RTGS (Real Time Gross Settlement) for time critical domestic and international payments. It transfers the gross/ full amount from one bank to another on real time / fast basis in batches throughout the day.

3. **CHIPS** (Clearing House Interbank Payments System) is the third major EFT method and again used in the US as a preferred mode of transferring money by Banks. It differs with Fedwire in following ways. 1. It is privately owned by Banks who are its members whereas Fedwire is part of the regulatory body (The Federal Reserve Bank of New York) and thus it's charges can be lower than those of Fedwire as beneficial to the member banks. 2. It is a netting engine instead of a gross engine and therefore not real time. It consolidates all the pending payments into fewer transactions. For example, If Citibank has to pay USD 1 Million to Bank of America

and Bank of America has to pay USD 0.85 Million to Citibank, CHIPS will aggregate these two payments into a single one and transfer only the net amount of USD 0.15 Mio from Citibank to Bank of America. Fedwire on the other hand would have made two separate payments for full amounts to Citibank and Bank of America.

In India, the payment and settlement systems are regulated by the Payment and Settlement Systems Act, legislated in December 2007.

The RBI has played a pivotal role in facilitating e-payments by making it compulsory for banks to route high value transactions (value of which exceeds INR 200,000/-) through RTGS and transactions of lower value by NEFT (National Electronic Funds Transfer) and NECS (National Electronic Clearing Services) which has encouraged individuals and businesses to switch to electronic methods of payment for remittances within India whereas SWIFT Network is used for foreign remittances.

Post demonetisation in India, the focus has increased on digital payments and Instant Money Transfer through banking channels like Immediate Payment Service (IMPS) and Mobile Money Identification Number (MMID)

The messages of transfer of money in all the above networks are formatted according to an applicable standard and encrypted for security and then the money (in form of a message) is sent from one bank to another.

Similar international transfers also occur when a person avails services like Western Union Money Transfer (that in turn transfers/ receives money from Bank), Credit Cards, PayPal, and international Travellers' Cheques etc.

In Money Laundering, wire transfers are used to remit black money from one location to another once it has been **smurfed** into the Bank Accounts. Let us see what smurfing means:

Smurfing means deposit of illegal cash in bank accounts in such a manner that suspicion is not aroused. Thus, the cash deposits are made in small amounts in multiple accounts.

Small amounts of cash deposit refers to amount beyond which identification proof is required by banks and/or a Cash Transaction report is sent to FIU for investigation.

Multiple Accounts can be of same entity or person in different banks and/or branches or of multiple entities (over which the black money holder holds beneficial interest) in the same bank and/or branches.

The Informal Way: Hawala Network

Hawala is also known as Alternate Remittance System or ARS internationally. Hawala is an Arabic word which means 'to transfer'. Here it means transfer of funds from one country to another.

The method is simple: If Mr Darkhorse, a black money holder based in New Delhi wants to send INR 20 Million of his black money in form of cash to his affiliate in Canada, he will approach Mr Jockey - an Angadia (which means *courier* in Hindi. He is also known as Hawaladar in this process). Mr Jockey takes the cash from Mr Darkhorse in New Delhi and sends a message to his network representative in Canada who then hands over the equivalent amount of U.S. or Canadian Dollars (less their commission) to Mr Darkhorse's affiliate in Canada.

There may be genuine requirements too of sending money abroad like settlement in a foreign country post retirement, medical treatment abroad and even charity overseas for which people trust and use the 'Hawala' mode of foreign remittance since there are no disclosure requirements in Hawala compared to stringent and full disclosure requirements under the normal banking channel. The method is fast too and trustworthy. The entire Hawala network works only on trust with no documentation.

Technically, it works as follows:

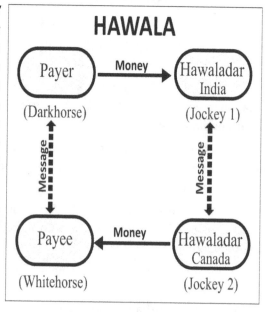

1. A customer 'Darkhorse' approaches a Hawala broker 'Jockey1' in New Delhi, India and gives a sum of money in Indian Currency (INR) that is to be transferred to a recipient 'Whitehorse' in Toronto, Canada. Along with the money, he usually specifies something like a password that will lead to the money being paid out.

2. Jockey1 calls another Hawala Broker - Jockey2 in Toronto, Canada and informs him about the agreed password or gives other disposition instructions of the funds.

3. He then informs Darkhorse about Jockey2's location and asks him to tell Whitehorse to meet him there.

4. Whitehorse is then informed by Darkhorse about the password and the contact details of Jockey2 in his city. Whitehorse approaches Jockey2 at the given location, informs the pass code and takes the money in equivalent Canadian Dollar (CAD) excluding a commission. Money remitted.

Jockey1 now owes money to Jockey2 and thus he trusts Jockey1's promise to settle the debt at a later date which he always does as is implied by the successful running of this system for decades. The off-setting leg of this transaction i.e. payment from Jockey1 to Jockey2 either happens through a similar Hawala transaction in reverse direction or by way of mispricing in International Trade, which we have covered in Trade Based Money Laundering (TBML) chapter.

Although this method is illegal but the network has been working since ages. With hundreds of foreign exchange related business doing rounds globally like money changers, tour operators, importers and exporters etc., only God knows who is part of this network and who is not.

The Crude Way: Cash Courier and Human Courier

You need to send money from India to Canada illegally, carry it yourself. Since this is illegal, it entails the risk of being caught. No country allows physical carrying of its currency outside its border beyond a permissible limit. Many money launderers get caught while doing so and subsequently become a news item. They carry physical cash/dollars, gold, diamonds or other precious stones from one country to another in this manner.

Similarly, launderers send physical cash through money orders, posts or international couriers too for the want of stringent KYC procedures in these modes.

Terrorists often use this method to transport currency from one country to another because even if it is caught, it is mostly counterfeit in nature. Hence they do not bear any significant loss.

Money Laundering is no magic

where

Black Money disappears and

White Money appears from nowhere

or

Money changes in its colour from black to white.

It is a process that requires documentation, time, knowledge and nexus to disguise the Black Money as White and prevent its forfeiture, penalty and prosecution.

The Methods and Modi Operandi

The methods of money laundering mentioned in this book are purely for academic interest.

Some of them existed in the past; some have been made practically redundant while some may still be existing.

Any such method requires deep expert knowledge for its explanation and deliberation. However they are explained here plainly and with simplicity so as to serve the interests of variety of readers in the matter.

No such explanation should be construed as an advice, opinion or professional view point.

METHOD 1

Colombian Peso Exchange

Colombian Peso Exchange was a much hyped traditional Money Laundering scheme that came into light in 1990s and was rampant for several decades before its popularity led investigators to kill it completely.

As we entered in 21st century, a lot has changed since then and money launderers have got modified version of this method perfectly incorporated into the TBML and the Hawala system of today. The modus operandi involved in this method thus remains interesting for academic purposes.

The modus operandi:

Peso is the currency of Colombia whose exchange here refers to exchanging Pesos with US Dollars. This is why the method is also known as 'Dollar Peso Exchange'.

Countries that were mainly involved in the scheme:

1. United States of America (USA or US)
2. Colombia

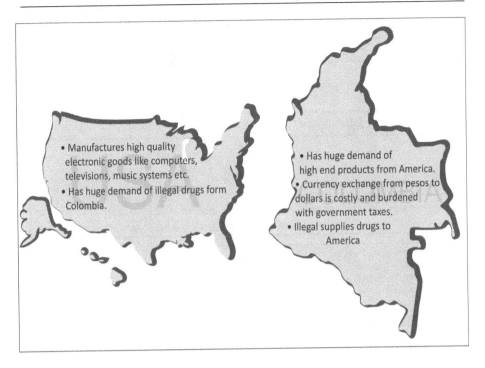

- Manufactures high quality electronic goods like computers, televisions, music systems etc.
- Has huge demand of illegal drugs form Colombia.

- Has huge demand of high end products from America.
- Currency exchange from pesos to dollars is costly and burdened with government taxes.
- Illegal supplies drugs to America

Participants in the scheme:

1. M/s Darkhorse& Co. – A Colombian drug cartel
2. M/s Jockey & Co. – A Colombian Peso Broker and Money Laundering Agent

    Both Darkhorse& Co. and Jockey & Co. run export-import business on paper and have operations in USA and Colombia

1. M/s Whitehorse & Co. – A Colombian Businessman
2. M/s American Business Co. – A USA Business Company.

    The Money Laundering scheme went as follows:

The Illegal drugs from Colombia are sold in the US by the employees / representatives of Darkhorse who accumulate US Dollars (Black Money).

The Black money is handed over to the representatives of M/s Jockey and Co. in the US

Representatives of M/s Jockey in the US deposit this cash in various ordinary accounts in small amounts through dozens of their smurfing agents to avoid <u>CTR</u> and <u>STR</u> reporting by Banks. These funds are then consolidated in a single account.

PS: CTR is filed by banks with financial intelligence unit of their country when cash transactions in an account exceed a threshold and STR is filed when they find any transaction to be suspicious with respect to money laundering.

M/s Whitehorse & Co. in Colombia wants to buy high end computers for his business from M/s American Business Co. (ABC)

M/s Whitehorse approaches M/s Jockey who specializes in import of US goods and charges lowest forex margin on conversion of pesos to dollars for import of computers from M/s ABC.
Whitehorse pays for the purchase in equivalent Pesos→Clean Money

The funds from the single bank in the US as mentioned above are used to pay to the American Business Co. which in turn ships the requisite computers to Whitehorse & Co. in Colombia

The pesos received from Whitehorse are transferred to Darkhorse to settle his account

Transactions settled. Money laundered

POINTS TO PONDER:

$ It is not possible to use this method in the current century because of the advancement in the extant Foreign Exchange and Anti-Money Laundering Laws.

$ However, this method gives us a glimpse of the background from where money laundering has evolved into a sophisticated business as on date.

METHOD 2

Layer of Trusted Lieutenants

This is one of the simplest, easiest and most widely used methods in disguising the source of black money earned by a person.

A trusted lieutenant can be any person whom the black money holder can trust to be a custodian of his property, either due to closeness with that person or undue influence over him or it may be due to ignorance/ illiteracy of that person.

It simply means that if people will suspect and link my holding of a certain amount of wealth and luxury with my wrong doing; then why should I hold that wealth (assets) in my name. Anyone who is trustworthy can hold the assets in his name with the benefits arising from such assets being enjoyed by me. This gives rise to the concept of beneficial ownership.

Such person can be anyone from my immediate or distant relatives, friends, clients, servants etc.

Let's take an example:

Mr Darkhorse has accumulated huge sums of money through his illegal activity of taking bribes for getting things done.

Now he has an obvious desire of enjoying his illegal income. He and his wife want to have big bungalow and a luxury car.

The problem is however that buying a luxury car and a house in his own name or in his wife's name would raise questions about their capacity of owing such high value assets being disproportionate to their legal income.

Further, there are statutory information reports required as per law that needs to be filed by the sellers (of apartment and car) with the Income Tax Department under the Income Tax Rules and on investigation of such reports, officials can trace him and he can go behind bars with all his black money confiscated.

Mr Darkhorse therefore thinks of a scheme:

$ For buying a car, he persuades his friend (say Mr Whitehorse) to buy a new car for him. Mr Whitehorse gratifying his friendship buys the car Darkhorse wants and then gives it to him for his beneficial use. What happens however behind the scene is that Mr Darkhorse gives his black money to Whitehorse who in turn buys the car for him by mixing the black money so received with his own white money. On papers therefore, Mr Whitehorse is the owner of the vehicle but it is used by Mr Darkhorse as and when required.

$ For buying a house, Darkhorse could have employed the same scheme as car but he uses a better one. He buys a flat in some developed outskirts of Mumbai in the name of some very old relative of his illiterate cook. The documents of the house are prepared in the name of such person who is extremely difficult to locate.

$ His cook, in return for some loyalty benefits, arranges some Identification document (like Voter ID Number) of his relative. Besides property documents, the will of that person is also prepared simultaneously which states that in event of his death, the property gets bestowed upon Mr Darkhorse (who is already cherishing the property as his farmhouse and plans to live there post retirement, away from public glare).

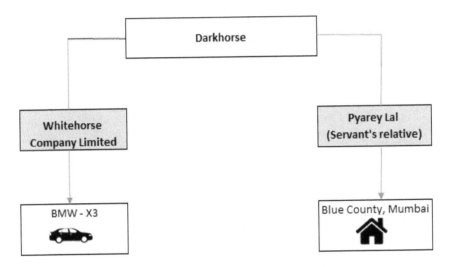

This method is used by black money holders to hold their black money assets in the names of people whom they can trust or who are simply gullible under their influence.

The above diagram shows Mr Darkhorse owning the assets through different entities.

Just like car and property (Bungalow), there can be other any other asset of which beneficial ownership is held by Darkhorse but not the real / legal ownership. Besides Will, there can be other documents for establishing beneficial ownership like Power of Attorney, Blank transfer deed (for securities) or there may be no document but absolute trust, influential or fiduciary relationship with the trusted lieutenant.

It may be noted that in real life scenarios, there will be more than one layer created by Mr Darkhorse between himself and the assets. There can be a servant, a client and a relative all involved in the chain of asset's title to complicate and disguise the source of black money.

Further, Mr Darkhorse would also want to apportion the assets purchased using his black money between different people and/or entities instead of putting all eggs in one basket. Thus, car could be in the name of one corporation, flat in the name of a servant, a business acting as cover or front in the name of an employee or relative and so on. Some assets and bank accounts can be even be situated abroad as we will see in later chapters/ sections.

POINTS TO PONDER:

$ Income Tax Department and other investigative agencies are fully aware of the use of trusted lieutenants/ nominees as a means of hiding black money. Because of its logical simplicity *(that Y has so much of money only because of his relationship with X)*, it does not take them long to get the ends meet and solve the case quickly.

$ Small evidence in support of beneficial interest or with respect to the flow of money or a recorded statement of the trusted person about the reality can land the money launderer into severe trouble.

$ Witnesses are easily found who will validate the usage of the ill-gotten assets by Mr Darkhorse and his family.

$ Annual Information Reports (AIR) of specified high value financial transactions are filed by various agencies under Indian Income Tax Rules disclosing the details of high value sales/ purchase transactions including property which help in investigating such transaction.

$ In India, the government is mulling to strictly apply the Benami *(meaning Anonymous)* Transactions Prohibition Amendment Act 2016 under which the government can confiscate the assets falling under beneficial ownership as well as penalise and prosecute people like Darkhorse with several years of jail term. Benami Properties, in simple terms refers to assets that are held in the name of 'Mr X' for which payment has been made by 'Mr Y'. After Demonetisation, the next big goal for the government should be to curb the Benami Properties. However, the challenge is that Land Records (which are important since large amount of black money resides in Real Estate) are not digitised and up to date in various parts of the country including Rural India where maximum population of the country resides. .

METHOD 3

Gifts

Simplest as it seems to be, this method states that if a person has got black money and he needs to convert that into white money; he just has to seek a gift of desired amount from a Whitehorse who is willing to depart his white money for a charge.

And what that willing person will get in return? It's the black money with premium☺☺.

For example: If Darkhorse has black money of INR 10 Mio that he needs to convert into white, all he has to do is to find a person who has surplus white money in his books of accounts and is willing to part with it for a commission.

The modus operandi:

Let me explain the modus operandi with a small story.

Mr Darkhorse works as a clerk in a City Development Authority.

He lives in a lavish bungalow, drives a luxury car and has all the luxurious mod-coms in his house. His complete lifestyle is an ostentatious display of wealth which by any means is far bigger and better than what his salary commands.

Taking a cue from his public display of assets, Income Tax Officials (ITO) come to search his house to check the source of his assets and the money he flaunts.

They are turned back by Darkhorse by showing them the gift deeds of all his enviable assets. ☹

To their surprise, he got them as gift from Mr Whitehorse who is his relative and they know him as a rich businessman of the city, big enough to easily part with the assets being flaunted by Darkhorse.

The actual picture that remains under wraps (although the tax officials would have unofficially noticed it in their first sight) is the modus operandi that worked behind these gifts.

Darkhorse had loads of black money – say INR 10 Million which he got as bribe. He gave this black money to his relative Whitehorse who in turn bought the assets (which Darkhorse wished for) from his white money and in his own name. He subsequently gifted them to Darkhorse through a gift deed. Money Laundered.

The black money of Darkhorse has become the black money of Whitehorse and which will be laundered again, making Money Laundering a circular and continuous process which keeps getting complex with every passing transaction.

Instead of buying assets, Whitehorse would have issued a cheque/wire transfer also in favour of Darkhorse for INR 10 Million against the black money received from him. The difference in both these cases being that of a robbery and a daylight robbery.

POINTS TO PONDER:

$ This method has been curbed by Indian Income Tax Act 1961 to a large extent. As per this law, all gifts, whether in cash or kind received by a person exceeding INR 50,000/- in any Financial Year are taxable as his 'Income from Other Sources' subject to certain exceptions.

$ Income Tax Act India taxes the gifts received by any person whether in cash or in kind (immovable or movable property, shares, securities, bullion, jewellery, paintings, drawings etc.) exceeding INR 50,000/-. However, no such gift is taxable if it is received:

  $ From a relative (the term relative is defined which includes many relatives of an individual)

  $ Or on occasion of his marriage

  $ Or under a Will

  $ Or from an Income Tax recognised trust or institution including charitable trusts etc.

  In case Mr Darkhorse is a businessman, 'gift' becomes a method of routing his black money into his business, through his relatives. There are other exceptions as well which still leave room for Money Laundering.

$ Accordingly, Darkhorses use the occasion of marriage (their own or their children's marriage) to convert their black money into white money where various invitees, friends and relatives gift piles of cash, gold and other precious items under pseudonyms to the bride or bridegroom. Darkhorses prepare and provide a well planned fictitious list to Income Tax Department with all details sought by it, making this Money Laundering tax free.

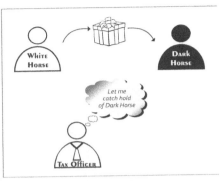 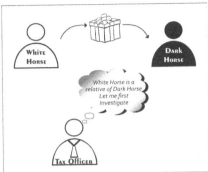

$ Since gifts from relatives are not taxable; Darkhorses also show huge amounts of white money received as gift from plethora of relatives (*within the scope of government approved definition*) on any occasion which they celebrated. For example: a family of four celebrates four birthdays, one marriage anniversary and various festivals in a Financial Year and receive gifts from relatives. However, all these gifts will be taxable in case proper details are not provided.

$ Further, if people like Darkhorses are lucky to have a Whitehorse kind of a relative who is a rich businessman, their nexus rides upon the system to launder funds as seen in the modus operandi in this chapter. It is therefore not a coincidence that some close relatives of many black money holders are rich businessmen and vice-versa. Their businesses start and flourish due to such black money. The government, however, is not just a spectator; the authorities can investigate all the deals between these parties and their organisations.

$ Trusts and institutions as mentioned above are also seldom used as a Money Laundering vehicle where modus operandi remains the same. Darkhorse gives his black money to an Income Tax recognised trust and receives a cheque/ wire transfer of equivalent amount (after deduction of commission) as a gift that becomes his white money. Obviously he took the trustees of such trust in confidence for mutual gains who will definitely face problem explaining the rationale of such act. The use of Charitable Trust in Money Laundering is detailed in a separate chapter.

$ Gifts from non-relatives attracts Income Tax but again if Darkhorse is so desperate for using his black money, he will launder it by showing it as collection of gifts received from numerous non-relatives and pay taxes on the amount

METHOD 4

Unsecured Loans

This is one of the simplest ways of laundering black money into white. Known by various names such as *Accommodation Entry, Bogus Loan or Jamakharchi Entry*, it is a darling of money launderers and entry operators. In common parlance, the method refers to exchange of cheque for cash (*'cash ke badle cheque'* in Hindi).

Because of its simplicity and effectiveness, this method is quite rampantly used in procuring white money. The method states that if someone does not have sufficient white money, he can always take a loan from someone who has it and there applies no restriction on the payer for being a relative of the payee as we saw in case of gifts.

A person having abundant black money who wants to convert it into white money finds either some acquaintance or some other person, firm, company etc. (through an agent) who has sufficient white money in his books of accounts and either wants to convert some of his white money into black or earn some good income on his white money.

Darkhorse who has got millions in black money and wants to invest a part of it in his business or for acquisition of property/real estate etc. in white money finds this method useful because of its effectiveness and low cost. Let us see how?

The modus operandi:

Mr Darkhorse has INR 1 Million of black money which he wants to convert into white money. He approaches Mr Jockey (an agent/ entry operator) who knows one Mr Whitehorse who has sufficient white money as surplus in his books of accounts and can part with that for some time to generate some income. Jockey assures Darkhorse of his best services and agrees to arrange white money for him at an interest rate of as low as 3% to 4% p.a. (tentatively) besides his commission.

Jockey convinces Whitehorse about the black money repayment capacity of Darkhorse and assures him that Darkhorse is committed to refund the loan amount either from his business profits that he will generate or from his various other alternate sources within a period of 1–3 years.

Whitehorse agrees to give loan of INR 1 Million to Darkhorse at an interest rate of say 12% p.a. (only for book entry purpose). How this interest rate of 12% p.a. converts into interest rate of 3% p.a. is another interesting story we will see here.

Whitehorse lends INR 1 Mio to Darkhorse in white and at the same time, Darkhorse gives his black money of INR 1 Million to Whitehorse. Money Laundered. Commission to Jockey is paid by Darkhorse.

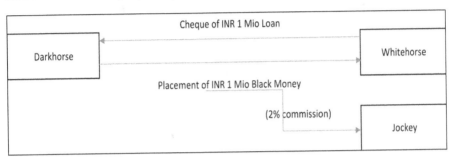

(Jockey may even facilitate this transaction through two or three Whitehorses instead of just one).

At the end of the Financial Year, Jockey obtains cheque (or wire transfer) for interest @12% p.a. from Darkhorse in favour of Whitehorse and takes black money from Whitehorse for differential rate of interest i.e. 9% p.a. This differential interest amount is given back to Darkhorse.

In this case, suppose the money was lent at the beginning of the Financial Year, so Darkhorse will pay INR 1,20,000 [12% x INR 1 Mio] to Whitehorse in white money and Whitehorse will return INR 90,000/- [9% x INR 1 Mio] back to Darkhorse in black money from the black money that was originally handed over to him. Thus the effective cost to Darkhorse comes only at 3% p.a. which was promised by Jockey.

Whitehorse earns this 3% on his white money whereas in reality, he has not lent anything except an Accommodation Entry since he has already received the equivalent amount in black money.

After utilizing INR 1 Mio in white money for the purpose for which it was required like buying of a house, car, machinery, obtaining bigger loan from Bank on the basis of higher white money or for any other business purpose etc.; Darkhorse will have to generate surplus white money in lump sum or in small amounts of say INR 1 Lakh (1/10 of 1 Million) plus interest for refunding the loan. The amounts can be smaller or larger than this depending upon the secret understanding between the parties. Repayment to Whitehorse can be in any form say in 10 or 20 equal or unequal instalments against which Mr Whitehorse will keep on returning the black money of equal amount to Darkhorse which was originally handed over to him.

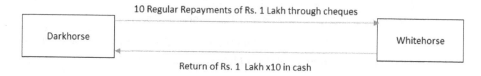

10 Regular Repayments of Rs. 1 Lakh through cheques

| Darkhorse | | Whitehorse |

Return of Rs. 1 Lakh x10 in cash

(1 Million = 10 Lakh)

This black money acts as a security to Whitehorse and is utilized by Whitehorse in his business or in lending to unorganised sector during this process earning higher rate of interest.

Not only does this method helps Darkhorse in using and generating white money by laundering his black money, it also gives him a tax advantage in from of deduction of interest expense @12% p.a. from his taxable white money.

The Agent - Jockey earns an approximate commission ranging from 0.50% to 3% on case to case basis of the total amount which he may or may not share with Mr Whitehorse depending upon the case. This commission is for facilitating the transaction, guaranteeing the credentials of the parties and undertaking paper work like book entries, loan confirmations etc. Such an agent can be anybody who is full-fledged dealing in Money Laundering or an accountant who is maintaining the books of accounts of both the parties.

Documents used:

Now let us have a look at some of the documents involved in the transaction:

At first stage where Whitehorse lends money to Darkhorse, Jockey obtains photocopies of Income Tax ID/ Permanent Account Number (PAN) and latest Income Tax Returns (ITR) of Whitehorse. PAN is a unique identification number provided by Income Tax Department in India.

When Darkhorse pays interest to Whitehorse, he deducts/ withholds tax as per the rules of Tax Deduction at Source (TDS) / Withholding Tax and submits an appropriate TDS certificate to Whitehorse that gives an authenticity to the whole transaction. Whitehorse on his part gives a Loan Confirmation Letter to Darkhorse that contains all the details of loan like the loan amount given, loan amount repaid, loan outstanding, interest paid etc. A **sample** of loan confirmation letter is depicted hereunder:

Loan Confirmation Letter

From,

Mr White Horse

123, White Road

Kolkata – 700123

West Bengal, India

To,

Mr Dark horse

456, Black Road

Kolkata – 700456

West Bengal, India

Sir,

Please confirm the following transaction for the period 01-04-15 to 31-03-16 (Assessment Year 2016-17)

(All amounts in INR)

01-Apr-15	**To Opening Balance**	**Nil**			
01-Apr-15	To Bank A/c Loan Given	10,00,000			
30-Sep-16	To Interest for 1st Half Year	60,000	30-Sep-16	By Bank A/c	54,000
			30-Sep-16	By Tax Deducted at Source on Interest @10%	6,000
31-Mar-16	To Interest for 2nd Half Year	60,000	31-Mar-16	By Bank A/c	10,54,000
			31-Mar-16	By Tax Deducted at Source on Interest @10%	6,000
			31-Mar-16	By Balance carried forward	Nil
	Total	**11,20,000**		**Total**	**11,20,000**

DH

Signed and Confirmed

Dark Horse

(PAN: ABCDE1234Z)

WH

Yours Faithfully

White Horse

(PAN: VWXYZ6789Z)

Now days, the ID proofs of people are scattered everywhere. Agencies and even individuals providing 3rd party (outsourcing) services to a credit card company, bank, telecom company etc. have become easy markets for the ID and Address Proofs of many gullible people.

When Jockey gets his hands on a photocopy of PAN Card of Mr A, he gets to know the following details mentioned thereupon – 1. PAN of A 2. Full Name of A 3. Date of Birth of A 4. Father's Name of A and 5. Specimen signatures of A.

Jockey knows how to abuse these details to create false loan documents that will show loan provided by Mr A to Darkhorse. Darkhorse then shows in his books of accounts that he has got the loan from Mr A whereas the money would be transferred into his account from somewhere else by Jockey.

In case, he knows that A is not an Income Tax payer, it becomes a boon for him.

Conclusion:

At the end of this transaction, Darkhorse receives back his black money.

People like Mr Jockey are always cunning. They try to misuse the Identification documents of innocent and unaware people. Then, there can be multiple small amounts loaned to Darkhorse by multiple people like Mr A. Darkhorse will use these loans for the purpose for which he wanted white money and then shave them off in his books after a period of time by generating white money in his books of accounts over a period of time through higher business proceeds by comingling of black money.

Jockey is undoubtedly clever enough to take care of the prohibition under Income Tax Act of India on receipt and payment of loans in cash over applicable threshold amount by supporting these accommodation entries through Bank Account statements, Identity Proofs, Loan Confirmations and other documentary evidences.

It may be noteworthy to point that instead of unsecured loans, these fictitious entries can take form of secured loans also but then it will require a lot more documentation and disclosure as well as various legal provisions related thereto shall apply like formalities for creation and satisfaction of such charge etc.

Therefore unsecured loans are used to avoid complications.

POINTS TO PONDER:

$ The Unsecured Loan method is still in use but has got a big blow from demonetisation scheme of Government of India.

$ There are lapses in the documentation with no proper loan agreement executed between the parties which can be exploited by the assessing officers of Income Tax Department (ITD) to catch hold of Darkhorses.

$ Unsecured Loans of the kind mentioned above are easily spotted by ITD.

$ The method may be surviving because of some anti law abiding jockeys who will be punished sooner or later bringing a slow death to this method but its modus operandi will always remain of academic interest.

METHOD 5

Assignment of Fixed Deposit (FD)

If Whitehorse has surplus funds in his bank accounts and he wants to lend them to Darkhorse, he will simply write a cheque in favour of Darkhorse or wire transfer the money into his account as seen in the previous chapter explaining Unsecured Loans. But what if Whitehorse, being an active fund manager has invested his funds (or for that matter, the funds of his firm, company, HUF etc.) in FDs with Bank(s)?

Answer: Whitehorse will give loan via assignment of his FDs.

That is what Whitehorse will do. He has sufficient white money and is willing to part with that money to Darkhorse for a commission but since the funds are invested in a FD, he will assign this FD in favour of Darkhorse.

Note that since it would be imprudent to take premature withdrawal of the Fixed Deposit Proceeds and forego the accrued interest thereon, Whitehorse will try to give loan without breaking his FD.

He does so by assignment of his FD in favour of Darkhorse

Assignment of FD simply means that all the rights, benefits and obligations emanating from that FD gets transferred from Whitehorse (assignor) to Darkhorse (assignee).

Modus Operandi:

Darkhorse has got INR 10 Million of black money which he wants to convert into white for use in his business or for acquisition of some big ticket assets.

He approaches Mr Jockey - a Bank Manager of Give And Take Bank say GAT Bank, who knows that one of his customers - Mr Whitehorse has got sufficient white money invested as FD in his Bank Branch.

Jockey convinces Whitehorse about the black money repayment capacity of Darkhorse and Whitehorse agrees to assign his FD of INR 10 Million in favour of

Darkhorse. The FD gets assigned in favour of Darkhorse and Whitehorse receives INR 10 Million in black money at the same time.

After the FD is assigned in favour of Darkhorse, Jockey gets a loan of INR 9.50 Million sanctioned to him from his GAT Bank after marking lien on the Fixed Deposit assigned to him. Simple lending for Jockey and Low Cost Borrowing for Darkhorse and his Money got laundered.

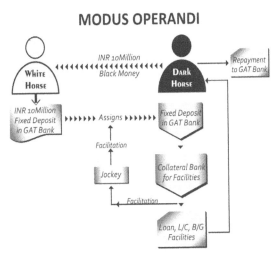

Needless to mention that both Jockey and Whitehorse get good commission for their support.

It may be noted that Jockey shall even facilitate sanction of an additional Bank Guarantee (BG) or Letter of Credit (LC) limit to Darkhorse if he wants to buy some goods or win a business contract backed by Bank LC or BG. The security being the same assigned FD.

The payment of the LC and BG will be done by Darkhorse from the loan sanctioned to him and the loan amount would be repaid either as per agreed terms or by redeeming the FD standing to his credit.

The method serves a good source of white money to Darkhorse who needs it for some expenditure or investment through his books of accounts (white money) when in reality his books do not show that much of money. Secondly, obtaining funds on loan provide an opportunity to generate required amount of white money gradually over time by comingling the black money with white money. We will see the mixing of white money with black money in detail in our chapter on Bogus Business/ Front Companies.

The reason why 'Loans' are used as a means to launder funds is two-fold:

First, it provides a shield in form of valuable and authentic documentation and

Second, it gives tax benefit on the amount of interest expense which is deductible from the taxable white money.

METHOD 6

Fake Creditors

In business terms, creditors are the vendors or suppliers who have provided some goods or services but are yet to be paid for those goods or services.

The method - Creation of fake creditors used in Money Laundering is again similar to receiving of unsecured loans since lenders are also a form of creditors.

If Mr Darkhorse, who has got millions in black money wants to use some part of it in his business without taking a loan from someone on paper, his other option is to straight away buy what he needs for his business be it Raw Materials, Capital Assets or some Services (through his black money) and then show them in his books as credit purchases or deferred credit purchases where payments are made in instalments over a period of time instead of one lump sum settlement.

The catch here is that the actual payment for such goods or services has already been made by Darkhorse in black money.

This gives rise to creditors in his books of accounts which are fictitious since payment to them has already been made in black money but appear in the Balance Sheet/ Financial Statements just to match the assets or expenditure incurred through black money.

Modus Operandi:

Darkhorse interested in his business expansion wants to buy INR 1 Mio worth of raw material from Whitehorse but is short of white money in his books of accounts to do that.

He connives with Whitehorse and buys the material through his black money but shows the same as credit purchase in his books of accounts. Whitehorse agrees as he sees no risk in it (after receiving his due amount in black money) and after all Whitehorse is his loyal customer.

Whitehorse accordingly, shows Darkhorse as his debtor in his books of accounts.

Subsequently, as we have seen in the case of Unsecured Loans, Mr Darkhorse will generate surplus white money in small amounts say INR 2 Lakhs or so and then settle the account with Whitehorse by payment from his white money who will hand over equal amount of black money to Darkhorse.

At the end of this transaction, Darkhorse receives back his black money.

METHOD 7

Donations to Political Parties

Donations to political parties are an important part of black money economy. The use of anonymity and pseudonyms as we saw in the chapter on Gifts is more extensive in the case of donations received by political parties.

In India, The Representation of People's Act 1950 and 1951 requires all the political parties to declare the details of all the donations/contributions received by them which are higher than INR 2,000/- (Prior to Union Budget 2017, this limit stood at INR 20,000). The political parties are required to disclose the donors' names, addresses and Permanent Account Numbers (PAN), if any if the amount of donation is higher than this limit.

Accordingly, these details are not required if the single donation amount is up to INR 20,000 till 31st March, 2017 and INR 2,000 thereafter which leaves ample scope for manipulation. This norm is flouted as many parties declare much of their donations below the threshold amount. Reduction of this threshold amount from INR 20,000/- to INR 2,000/- is not very significant since only the number of donors will get changed. Previously a donation amount was split in denominations less than INR 20,000; now that will be split in denominations of less than INR 2,000. Many political parties already show donations of paltry amounts from numerous donors.

The practice of selling electoral tickets by political parties to candidates who provide political parties with humongous sums of black money is also no secret.

Here the government has made an impact through Union Budget 2017 which says that no person shall receive an amount of 300,000/- or more in cash in aggregate from any other person (subject to certain exceptions but not including political parties in such exceptions) in a single day or with respect to a single transaction or event or occasion. Thus the recipients of money from political parties will face some heat due to this provision.

However, the catch is that since there is no tax payable by political partie their income, be it from donations or otherwise, they are free to deposit any amou of cash in their bank accounts in the garb of donations.

Political parties use money for various purposes – for organising rallies, transporting people from one place to another, hiring vehicles of all sorts including private jets and helicopters, hiring places, equipments, advertisements, distribution of kickbacks, freebees and everything required to win votes.

But still, because of the various privileges available to political parties, there remains scope of Money Laundering. Let us see how:

A political party is created and registered under Representation of People's Act, 1951. (It is not even mandatory for these parties to contest elections and even if they do contest, they are not required to win).

Black Money is donated to this political party in small parts, each donation being less than INR 2,000/-. There being no limit on number of such donations/ transactions.

All this black money is deposited in the party's bank account. There is no tax on these donations/ income of political parties.

Now the money is available for withdrawal from the party's bank account as and when desired. Money Laundered. Since Right to Information Act does not apply on political parties (barring a few major ones), RTI application asking source of donations less than INR 2,000/- from political parties cannot be filed.

POINTS TO PONDER:

$ An Income Tax Officer has the power to question the source of donations from political parties.

$ Electoral reforms like funding of elections only through state or central exchequers and stringent monitoring of the expenditure is suggested by many experts to provide a big boost in this area.

METHOD 8

Charitable Trusts

*I*f you wonder how she is able to travel so much and work so little at such a young age, it is because her parents set up a trust that provides for most of her living expenses.

A trust is a legal entity created by a party (the trustor) through which a second party (the trustee) holds the right to manage the trustor's assets or property for the benefit of a third party (the beneficiary).

Here property interest is held by a party (the trustee) for the benefit of another (the beneficiary).

In case the objective of the trust is to provide education, relief to the poor, medical relief or advancement of any other object of public utility, then such trust becomes a charitable trust in Indian law and enjoys full tax exemption on its incomes (donations, revenues etc.) provided it has spent more than a threshold amount of its income say 85% of its income for the purposes for which it got established. It can thus accumulate only up to 15% of the income for future spending which is not a difficult proposition to fulfil and is the only major condition to avail tax exemption.

Tax benefits are available to charitable trusts because of the public services they are entrusted upon. However, some of the charitable trusts are not trustworthy.

Here, the amount that goes to trust in form of donations/ contributions etc. is used for purposes which are although different from the purposes for which the trust was established but do not appear to be so technically. For example: Darkhorse donates INR 1 Million of his black money to a charitable trust. The charitable trust comingles this money with its white money. It buys a SUV car for its mission on paper but that car is used by Darkhorse for his personal purposes (not when the trust audit is going on). The trust is exempt from tax on this donation. Full Money Laundering, tax free.

Similarly, donation is given to construct a new building for purposes of trust on which tax exemption is claimed. The building gets constructed and some of the spare/ unused rooms in the building are given on rent. The rent goes to Darkhorse in cash and the same is not recorded in the books of the trust. Partial Money Laundering, tax free.

The new Companies Act of India requires certain companies to spend a certain percentage (~2%) of their average net profits on Corporate Social Responsibility (CSR). This provision although introduced to achieve social development, is often misused by corporates.

Social Welfare Projects in India are mostly administered by Non-government Organisations (NGOs) that are constituted as charitable trusts. Therefore, corporates often donate funds to NGOs for carrying out social development and claim such expenditure as CSR spending. Although many NGOs are reputable and actually work for the betterment of the society, there are some NGOs which are created for deception and abuse. Some of these second category NGOs have been found to have political connections.

Many NGOs are informally organised and work with little governance. Therefore, the use of funds by these NGOs often cannot be monitored or audited. This advantage is taken by the NGOs backed by political parties as they act as means of collecting political donations, dispensing patronage or circumventing election laws.

Therefore, in the name of CSR, sometimes corporates donate funds to such NGOs and in return the beneficiary political party provides such corporates with various advantages as they may have agreed upon. Advantages may include helping in various ways like acquisition of land, grant of a business contract, grant of a license, lobbying for the company in various forums etc.

The donor corporate gets tax benefit on its donation, its CSR responsibility gets fulfilled and a connection with a political party is also formed. All at one go.

Electoral Trusts:

Corporates and industrialists often prefer using Electoral Trusts in order to channel their funds to a political party. An electoral trust is basically a trust created as per law, with the objective of receiving voluntary contributions from various sources and distributing such contribution to political parties.

Income (Donations, Contributions) of Electoral Trust are exempt provided it has spent more than a threshold amount of its income say 95% of its income for the purposes of giving donation to political parties (like it was 85% for charitable trusts).

Such trust acts as a curtain for the corporates as their name does not get associated with any political party. Donations given to electoral trusts are exempt from tax and the actual donor remains anonymous. With this political parties may bypass the legal requirement of disclosing the details of the donor. They will disclose only the details of the electoral trust as donor and not the person who is donating to this electoral trust.

The donor, the trust and the political party all are exempt from payment of tax on this amount.

Thus a political party is directly and indirectly financed by the government in three ways:

1. By not charging Income Tax in respect of income of political parties.
2. By not charging Income Tax in respect of donations/ income of electoral trust distributing its money to political parties.
3. By not charging Income Tax in respect of any sum contributed by Indian company to any political party.

For example:

An Indian company with an income of INR 10 Million decides to contribute INR 100,000 to 'XYZ' political party. It saves Tax at the rate of 33% (including cess) on its net outflow of contribution that comes out to be 33% of INR 100,000. When political party receives this INR 100,000, it again does not have to pay any tax over it. The government loses INR 33,000 and who knows if a political party is able to garner more donations just because of this clause. If a political party has black money, it may take donation from a corporate (white money) and return the amount in black money after deduction of a commission, all facilitated by the legal provisions. It encourages donations, it encourages tax avoidance and it encourages Money Laundering.

It may be noted that even in the wake of demonetisation in India, there were instances where many political parties deposited large amounts of cash in their party accounts since they are not liable to any tax on the same. Who knows if this privilege is misused by them to launder black money into white or not as explained above.

METHOD 9

Earning Agricultural Income

To keep poor farmers out of the tax ambit and its compliance as well as to encourage agricultural production, agricultural income is completely exempt from taxation in India and similarly in various other countries.

However, this leaves a loophole open for the money launderers to play their dirty games.

Exemption of agricultural income means income from sale of agricultural produce like pulses and cereals etc. is completely exempt from tax and so is the income from sale of agricultural land.

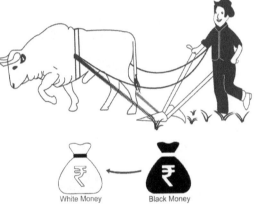

White Money   Black Money

The modus operandi:

Mr Darkhorse who has huge amount of black money uses a part of it in buying an agricultural land (majority of the purchase price is again paid through black money). He then shows income from sale of pulses and other commodities from the farmland on a regular basis even unaffected by rains and/or drought.

There is a good degree of probability that some of the relatives / servants / other acquaintances of Darkhorse would be owning some ancestral agricultural land and they would be more than happy to transfer it to Darkhorse for good enough sales consideration.

Since the land records of agricultural property (commonly known as 'khasra' and 'khatauni' in India) are poorly maintained (mostly through manual entries), there is much scope of manipulation in the same.

Darkhorse, if he so desires makes use of his connections and money power to back date the land acquisition transaction which enables him to declare higher revenue.

Once the agricultural land is bought, revenue from the agricultural produce is shown through an arrangement of fictitious receipts from numerous commodity brokers.

There are various intermediaries and commodity brokers who buy the produce from the farmers and sell it in open markets. They issue receipts to these farmers for the quantity and amount of agricultural produce bought from them. Darkhorse demonstrates his money power to gain from the ignorance and illiteracy of poor farmers and obtains various fictitious receipts from these commodity brokers in his own name. Such receipts are then used to declare his black money in the garb of white money. Money Laundered tax free.

Darkhorse can also sell his agricultural land to some Whitehorse once his purpose is fulfilled or if he wants to launder a big chunk of black money at one go. In such a case, the land is sold to Whitehorse at a huge premium taking benefit of the law which states that all gains including Capital Gains from agricultural land are exempt from tax. Money Laundered tax free.

POINTS TO PONDER:

$ The non-taxability of agricultural income definitely leaves scope for laundering of black money but the quantum is significantly restricted.

$ To complicate the matters for investigators, the farm land is acquired in the far flung areas, beyond the easy accessibility of tax officers.

$ However a tax officer can always ask Mr Darkhorse how he sold so much of rice or oranges and that too at a price higher than the market. Similarly, every land has a capacity to production too. The officer is sure to get some fruits instead of a satisfying answer.

METHOD 10

Real Estate

Real Estate signifying land, building and business related thereto like acquisition, construction, development, transfer etc. is one of the biggest markets of black money.

There is following semblance between real estate and black money:

- ✓ Both black money and real estate Transactions lack transparency.
- ✓ Both black money and real estate transactions involve significant cash.
- ✓ Both black money and real estate are organised games played by rich and influential persons.
- ✓ Criminality and power play a significant role in both black money and real estate Transactions.

Leave aside big developers and visit office of any property dealer in the city and you are sure to find a big vault with a circular lock somewhere in the office to store large amounts of cash. This symbolises the significance which cash enjoys in this industry.

Some of the other factors that I would like to highlight with respect to the use of black money in Indian Real Estate industry are as follows

✓ In India, with rapid urbanisation, pressure on land acquisition has been paramount. Since land is short in urban areas, builders try to acquire land from bordering areas which is usually agricultural in nature. Agricultural land in India generally refers to land located after 8 kilometres of a municipality or cantonment board limit which means that it is not too far from Business Districts in metropolitan cities and therefore eyed for acquisition by all shrewd real estate players.

✓ Acquisition of such land mostly happens in black money. Farmers and other land owners prefer black money as it helps them in relocation and avoids reporting.

✓ Next step is change of land use from agricultural to commercial, industrial or residential which is again enveloped in black money since the government servants fully aware of the above game want to make hay while the sun shines.

✓ Then comes in arrangement of urban infrastructure including electricity connection, water connection, building plan approval, drainage connection, construction of service roads etc. which are all mired in corruption and black money. Payment to contractors and labourers is just a small issue in front of all this.

✓ Since the labour and materials are sourced from unorganised sector, the scope of inflation of expenses and under reporting of profits is very significant.

✓ Floor Area Ratio (FAR) or Floor Space Index (FSI) which is the ratio of a building's total floor area (gross floor area) to the size of the piece of land upon which it is built is also open to various interpretations at various levels facilitating use of black money to obtain approvals.

✓ The Accounting Standard (AS)–7 or IndAS-11 corresponding to IAS-11 (IFRS 15 is set to replace IAS-11 in some time) which prescribes Percentage of Completion Method for revenue recognition from Construction Contracts, in most cases, fails to include Real Estate Developers under its scope for one reason or another like no reliable measurement of project cost and/or project revenue and/or stage of completion.

When their industry operates in a shadow, it is difficult to blame developers for accepting sales consideration in black money. 😊

The developers welcome customers who want to pay through black money as it helps them in booking lower sales revenue, thereby lowering their taxes and secondly helps them in undertaking illicit expenditures.

Let us now look at the Modus Operandi used in Real Estate sector to launder Black Money into white:

Modus Operandi 1: Use of Circle Rates

Circle rates are the property rates usually defined by the local state governments or the local development authorities, in line with what they perceive as the price at which sale or purchase of property should take place in a region. Since these rates are notified area wise or circle wise, they are known as circle rates. The purpose of notifying these rates is to determine the amount of stamp duty payable to government on the transfer of property.

Stamp Duty is payable at the actual transaction price or the Circle Rate price, whichever is higher. In India, the stamp duty is generally paid by the buyer.

For example:

Property	100 sq. yard of plot
Circle Rate of a Property	INR 10,000/- per square yard
Stamp Duty Rate in the state	6%
Scenario 1	
Deal Rate 1	INR 12,000/- per square yard
Stamp Duty payable on transfer	INR 72,000/-
	(6% x 12,000/- x 100 square yard)
Scenario 2	
Deal Rate 2	INR 8,000/- per square yard
Stamp Duty payable on transfer	INR 60,000/-
	(6% x 10,000/- x 100 square yard)
	Thus Stamp Duty payable is INR 60,000/- instead of INR 72,000/- since the Circle Rate is higher than actual rate in this case.

Extending this example to understand the psychology of Buyer and Seller in a sale-purchase transaction:

Suppose the market rate of the aforementioned plot is INR 18,000/- per square yard.

In such case, the buyer of said 100 square yard plot may not be willing to prepare the conveyance/ sale deed @ 18,000/- per square yard because he will have to bear the stamp duty of INR 108,000/- (6% x 18000 x 100 sq. yard) whereas if the transaction is registered at Circle Rate of INR 10,000/- per square yard, he would save INR 48,000/- on this deal by paying stamp duty of only INR 60,000/- as stated above.

Moreover, even if the buyer is willing to bear this additional burden of stamp duty, the seller may not be willing to sell it for a higher amount because he will then have to pay more tax due to higher amount of Capital Gain.

Thus it is a win-win situation for both parties to conceal the true sale consideration. More so for the seller since he saves capital gains tax.

Note: As per Indian Income Tax Act 1961, if sale of the property is at a price lower than Circle Rate then the difference between the Circle Rate and the sale price will be deemed as income of the seller. For example, If Seller shows that he sold 100 sq. yard plot at INR 800,000/- whereas the Circle Rate of this land is INR 1,000,000/- (@ INR 10,000/- per square yard). Then INR 200,000/- will any way deemed to be the income of the seller over and above his actual profit. Therefore, seller would not want to sell his property at a price lower than Circle Rate unless the market rate is really lower than the Circle Rate which is generally not the case.

This method is exploited when the market rates are much higher than the circle rates.

Coming back to the Modus Operandi:

Darkhorse has INR 1,000,000/- (1 Million) of surplus black money which he fears can either get seized by tax authorities or may get spent on unnecessary expenses.

Therefore he buys a property from Whitehorse through a property agent Jockey. The details are hereunder:

Property	150 square yard plot of land
Circle Rate of a Property	INR 9,000/- per square yard
Deal rate (Now)	INR 16,000/- per square yard
Actual Purchase Price	INR 2,400,000/- (16,000*150 square yard)
Sale Deed Registered with State Government @ Circle Rate	INR 1,350,000/- (9,000*150 square yard)
Amount paid in white money	INR 1,350,000/-
Amount paid in black money	INR 1,050,000/- (2,400,000 – 1,350,000)

- ✓ Thus Darkhorse transferred his black money to Whitehorse who will be laundering it further.
- ✓ This method requires Darkhorse to involve some of his white money also but that's not a difficult proposition for someone who can generate huge sums of black money.

When the market price of this property appreciates or if required earlier, Darkhorse sells this plot and converts his black money into white by asking full amount in white money as follows:

Deal Rate in Future (Assuming no appreciation)	INR 16,000/- per square yard
Actual Sale Price	INR 2,400,000/- (16,000*150 square yard)
Amount received in white money	INR 2,400,000/-

Black Money laundered: INR 1.05 Mio (INR 2.4 Mio – INR 1.35 Mio). In practice, this amount can vary on case to case basis depending upon Darkhorse's liquidity position, willingness of buyer for payment in white money, need of funds, appreciation in the real estate market, willingness of seller to pay tax on entire book profit etc.

Modus Operandi 2: Use of Section 54 of Indian Income Tax Act 1961

Reinvestment in Real Estate

Besides above, there is an additional factor that legally facilitates Money Laundering in this sector. There is a provision in Indian Income Tax Act which exempts Long Term Capital Gains (LTCG) arising from sale of residential real estate property from tax subject to a condition that Capital Gain proceeds are reinvested into new residential real estate property.

LTCG here means capital gain arising from sale/transfer of a residential property which has been held for at least 2 years post acquisition (This time limit has been reduced to 2 years by Union Budget 2017 from 3 years existing previously).

The enabling provision is contained under section 54 of Income Tax Act 1961. It exempts from tax, any LTCG arising from sale of a residential property (be it an apartment, bungalow, house or residential plot of land) if the amount of profit (i.e. Capital Gain) is reinvested into purchase of another residential property that is held for a period of 3 years. In case of residential plot however, one needs to construct a building within three years from date of acquisition.

As the provision requires only the Capital Gain amount to be reinvested, and not the full sale proceeds, it enables conversion of black money into white in a tax free way.

Let us see by way of an example:

Darkhorse bought a bungalow of INR 50 Million by paying INR 25 Million in black money and balance INR 25 Million in white money.

Let's say, after 3 years (or even 2 years) Darkhorse approaches Jockey who is a property dealer in the market and asks him to sell this bungalow to someone who pays full amount in white. Jockey knows that there are two types of buyers in this property market –

1. Black Money Hoarders who want to park their black money in real estate.
2. Genuine investors or end users who will use their hard earned white money to buy their dream house.

Jockey finds Mr Whitehorse who falls under the 2nd category mentioned above. He agrees to buy the black money bungalow of Darkhorse by paying full amount through cheque / bank transfer after some negotiation.

Assuming that there is no appreciation in the price of the Darkhorse's bungalow even after 3 years and the sale price remains same at INR 50 Million. *(This period can be 2 years also since post Budget 2017, sale of an immovable property purchased more than 2 years ago gives rise to Long Term Capital Gain or Loss)*

Darkhorse gets INR 50 Mio in white. Money Laundered but this sale attracts LTCG tax under Income Tax Act on Capital Gain of INR 25 Mio (INR 50 Mio sale price – INR 25 Mio purchase price in white)

It may be noted that there would be some indexation factor also due to long term holding of the asset.

Assuming the indexation benefit is nominal at 5% for 3 years, the Capital Gain amount is 95% of INR 25 Mio = INR 23.75 Mio.

To launder this money tax free, Darkhorse keeps aside INR 26.25 Mio with himself and reinvests INR 23.75 Mio into another residential real estate unit for a period of 3 years.

After 3 years, even if he sells his property for INR 23.75 Mio (assuming no appreciation and hence no Capital Gain), he has effectively laundered all his black money of INR 25 Mio which he had initially without paying even a penny of Income Tax. Money Laundered tax free.

Moreover, it is highly unlikely that a residential property, carefully selected by Darkhorse and Jockey for long term investment will not appreciate after 3 years.

Let us examine this case once again, assuming a modest10% appreciation in 3 years:

Property (Residential) -1	500 square yard plot of land
Darkhorse buys the residential property:	
Circle Rate of a Property	INR 50,000/- per square yard
Deal rate(Buy)	INR 100,000/- per square yard
Actual Purchase Price	INR 50,000,000/- (100,000*500 square yard)
Sale Deed Registered with State Government @Circle Rate	INR 25,000,000/- (50,000*500 square yard)
Amount paid in white money	INR 25,000,000/-
Amount paid in black money	INR 25,000,000/-
Darkhorse sells the residential property-1:	
Actual Deal Rate (Sale) (Assuming 10% appreciation)	INR 110,000/- per square yard
Actual Sale Price	INR 55,000,000/- (110,000*500 square yard)
Amount received in white money	INR 55,000,000/-
Long Term Capital Gains Taxable (assuming 10% indexation benefit)	INR 27,500,000 (55,000,000 – 25,000,000*1.10)
Tax payable @ 20%	INR 5,50,000/-
Darkhorse reinvests the profit in another residential property -2:	
Property (Residential) -2	2800 square feet apartment
Actual Deal rate (Buy)	INR 10,000/- per square feet
Actual Purchase Price (White)	INR 28,000,000/- (10,000 * 2800 square feet)
Amount taxable in the hands of Darkhorse	Nil, if he keeps his investment for next 3 years.
$ Money Laundered without any penny of tax implication. Even there is scope of laundering further black money while reinvesting the Capital Gain proceeds.	

Those of you who keep on thinking why the Indian property market is so immune to the forces of demand and supply, the above provides a reason to ponder.

Thanks to their black money, people like Darkhorse have huge holding capacity without any need for appreciation. Any investment opportunity that enables parking off their black money makes them happy. Real Estate is therefore considered a better investment avenue by Darkhorses of India unless their wives and daughters are after them.

Further, with Indian and International governments joining hands in curbing the offshore stashing of black money, the black money being generated in India and that coming from overseas is getting invested mainly in Real Estate and Gold.

Modus Operandi 3: Use of Real Estate as collateral to obtain loan

Mr Darkhorse has got huge amount of black money amassed which he wants to put to use and launder.

He therefore turns to real estate industry for his rescue. He becomes a builder or a developer i.e. buying, selling, developing land, houses, properties etc. becomes his business objective.

The benefit he derives from this activity is two-fold. One, real estate industry offers ample room for using his illegitimately obtained black money as seen in the previous two modi operandi. Second, he even gets good returns in this business. Eventually he may even start focusing more on his real estate business rather his original one.

In this endeavour of his, a factor that helps Darkhorse even more is use of his real estate assets as collateral for obtaining loan from banks/financial institutions.

Darkhorse for example has acquired a piece of real estate worth of INR 50 Mio by using INR 25 Mio of his white money and INR 25 Mio of black money (i.e. comingling).

After some time, he gets this property valued by a registered valuer of government department who has no problem in valuing this property at INR 50 Mio. He will even state that he is being conservative and is not considering any appreciation.

Darkhorse uses the said valuation to obtain a loan of INR 30 Mio from a Bank/ Financial Institution against this asset. Banks are also happy to get a secured loan business. The loan will be repaid from comingled black and white revenue from this business. Money Laundered tax free.

Any guesses in which business he would be using this loan. You are right – Real Estate. Rest assured, you have got to know one of the reasons behind the boom and bubble of the Real Estate Industry and you would now notice that it's for no insane reason that many businesses that had nothing to do with real estate initially moved to this business making it an additional business vertical.

Modus Operandi 4: Forfeiture of Booking Amount

As discussed, many real estate companies deal with black money incredibly. They may therefore use their pool of black money to help someone else requiring black money or loss (to evade tax) and earn commission in doing so.

Example: Mr Whitehorse is owner of M/s ABC Property Consultants and wants to show INR 1 Million of business losses to avoid payment of tax. Thus he wants of black money in lieu of his white money. He approaches XYZ Construction Company owned by Mr Darkhorse for this purpose. Darkhorse agrees to help Whitehorse for an agreed commission. He asks Whitehorse to book 5 flats in this under construction building. The sale price of 1 flat is INR 20 Million and booking price is INR 200,000/- i.e. 1% of the sale price. There is also a condition that if the booking is cancelled, the booking amount will be forfeited. Whitehorse agrees. He books 5 flats of value INR 100 Million by paying INR 1 Million in white through cheque or wire transfer.

Subsequently, citing certain excuses, Whitehorse cancels his bookings in XYZ Construction Company to which effect his INR 1 Mio of booking amount is forfeited by the company.

However, what happens off-records is that Mr Darkhorse of XYZ Construction returns INR 1 Mio to Whitehorse in black money after deduction of his commission as per their secret understanding. Money Laundered.

Whitehorse gets a loss of INR 1 Mio in his books of accounts on which he will save tax. Darkhorse gets his commission.

Such kind of bogus sales and purchase entry is not restricted to Real Estate businesses. It is exploited by all sorts of businesses. Pay in white for your purchases and take nothing in return except cash or other form of black money. In effect you have lent a bogus sales entry for a commission and recorded a bogus purchase entry. It is done in reverse manner when someone needs white money against his black money.

Modus Operandi 5: Loan as Sales

Mr Whitehorse, a lender businessman has lent huge amount to XYZ Construction Company of Mr Darkhorse. However, this transaction is not visible from the financial statements of XYZ Construction Company or even from those of Whitehorse's statements.

Reason: The loan amount received by XYZ has been recorded as sales. Got it? OK, Here are the fine details:

Suppose, Whitehorse has lent INR 1 Mio to XYZ Construction Company on interest rate of 14% p.a. but all this is off-records and stated in some unofficial/ secret memorandum of understanding.

This amount of INR 1 Mio is shown by XYZ as sales and an apartment of INR 10 Mio is booked in the name of Whitehorse showing INR 1 Mio as booking amount or instalment paid amount. Whitehorse gets a flat in his name. He is secured.

XYZ gets to increase its sales in its books of accounts without recording the actual loan. This enables the company to negotiate higher loan or better terms for its existing loans with its Banks/ Financial Institutions.

Whitehorse too records the amount lent as investment in his books of accounts instead of Loan advanced.

Subsequently, Whitehorse is paid the interest amount in black money and his booking gets cancelled. The apartment comes back to XYZ and Whitehorse gets back his principal amount in white. There may be some fictitious forfeiture also as stated in previous modus operandi, if Whitehorse wants to book loss and evade tax. He is anyways not going to pay tax on the interest earned in black money. Both won at the cost of government's exchequer. Money Laundered.

POINTS TO PONDER:

$ Central and State Governments need to work together to align circle rates with market rates and make the process of circle rate notification quite dynamic.

$ Demonetisation in India has already taken a toll on real estate industry. However more measures are required to delink this industry with black money.

METHOD 11

Doing Bogus Business/Front Companies

Ever noticed some businesses where no customer seems coming but still the office, shop, restaurant, hotel etc. keep running for years and continue surviving. Notice more closely and you may find Money Laundering to be a reason behind these businesses.

Some businesses are mere fronts – businesses created to hide and disguise the actual source of money.

People who have black money and want to use it without being caught generally try to show it as a business income. Under this method, the illegal and illegitimate money they have got is blended with the money coming from a legitimate business so as to make the black money appear legitimate and genuine to the maximum extent.

For example: Mr Darkhorse may decide to open a new restaurant with his white money and borrowings from Bank. Although it is found empty on most occasions but has great occupancy rates on paper and the money is deposited in its bank accounts on a regular basis.

To eliminate suspicion arising from low foot falls, Darkhorse might buy an existing restaurant that is running successfully. It helps him in three ways:

- ✓ The successful running of the restaurant makes it easy to deposit higher amount of black money in bank accounts in the garb of business proceeds.
- ✓ The skilled and talented staff of the restaurant will be retained that will help its success to continue.
- ✓ Much of the purchase consideration to acquire this business would be paid in black money enabling laundering of a big chunk of black money at one go.

Doing a bogus business is thus a key method to launder money. Businesses that deal extensively in cash or have solid inflows of revenue and obscure relationship with inventory and expenditure (to trace the flow of black money into business) are more prone to be used for this purpose.

It may be noteworthy to point here that the name 'Money Laundering' got coined in United States of America (USA) when the businesses of public laundries and Laundromats there was exploited extensively by the money launderers.

Some of the businesses vulnerable to this kind of a game are:

$ Restaurants

$ Fast Food Joints

$ Bars and Nightclubs

$ Confectionary Stores

$ Grocery Stores

$ Parking Lots

$ Currency Exchanges

$ Laundries

$ Transport Companies

$ Software Companies

$ Services and Consultancy firms

$ Toy companies

$ Trading - Import Export Business (as elaborated in Trade Based Money Laundering chapter)

Mr Darkhorse will show bogus sales, over invoice his sales, under-invoice his expenditures (difference being paid through his black money) and in this way inflate his revenue and profit to account for his black money. For example: The actual sales from business are INR 100 and expenses are INR 60 and thus his profit is INR 40. He manipulates the sales as INR 105 and reduces the expenses to INR 55 showing his net profit as INR 50 which enables him to deposit INR 10 of his black money along with actual profit of INR 40 in his bank account.

Carrying bogus business also provides Darkhorse a source of income for buying a luxury car, a luxury villa and other such assets either in his own name or in the name of his business entity. When purchased under the name of his business, Darkhorse also enjoys tax benefit on depreciation as well as on running expenses of such assets.

For example: If Darkhorse buys a Toyota Lexus car from the accounts of his front company – Genuine Business Private Limited (GBPL), he can avail depreciation, fuel, repair and maintenance and driver cost as expenditures in the accounts of GBPL and hence will get tax benefit on all these expenditures.

There has been a software tool that has been misused in the past by businesses. A tool that allows promoters of big companies to alter the accounting records of the company so as to facilitate Money Laundering is – Trojan Horse. Trojan Horse is a backdoor gateway to a software (say accounting software in this case) that is known to only a select few. It is created deliberately by the software company to provide a hidden access to a select few.

Trojan Horse comes to use when hundreds of employees of a company are working in its Accounting and Finance department keeping an eye over every penny of company's money. In such a case, a promoter enters into the accounting software secretly by using his ID and Password and places entries in the business accounting software directly without following any internal procedures which are otherwise applicable for every voucher. Although the effect of such entries would be clearly visible but the bare entries would not be visible to everyone. The matter will be escalated to the management but eventually closed abruptly without much disclosure.

These entries would be mostly related to fictitious sales, revenue from which will be a cover up for the black money of the promoter. Since no employee knows this secret, there is no risk of any whistle blower in this case.

POINTS TO PONDER:

$ Tax authorities can easily find that a business has started showing significantly higher revenue after it has been taken over by Darkhorse. The reasons behind this spike can be investigated further.

$ Cash Transaction Report and Suspicious Transaction Reports are filed by Banks with Financial Intelligence Unit (FIU) if the cash deposits are more than a threshold (say INR 1 Mio in a year) or if the transactions arise any suspicion in the minds of bankers with respect to money laundering. FIU then investigates all these transactions in detail.

METHOD 12

Shell Corporations

A Shell Company or a shell corporation is a corporation without active business operations or significant assets. Such company is not active in business and its assets may not be commensurate to the size of its business. Some shell companies may have had operations in the past, but those may have shrunk due to unfavourable market conditions, company mismanagement, takeover of assets, demerger of assets etc. A shell corporation may also exist even when its operations have been wound up, but still the "shell" of the original company continues to survive.

These types of corporations are not illegal *per se* but it's their use that can be illegitimate so as to disguise business ownership from law enforcement or the public. Shell companies may also be used to carry the bogus business as discussed in the previous chapter on Doing Bogus Business/Front Companies.

The relationship of Shell Corporations and Money Laundering is akin to that of bread and butter or that of fuel and car. Shell corporations can be located both onshore (within India) and offshore (outside India) stashed with wealth - black and white and sitting at the junction between these two economies that drive each other.

On-shore and offshore shell companies are used either independently or collectively to fuel the vehicle of Money Laundering. They keep cycling white money to black and black money to white.

Method 12.1: On-Shore Shell Companies:

Shell companies in India are known as Investment companies, 'Jamakharchi' companies and even 'Calcutta' companies as they have become an organised business in Kolkata (erstwhile Calcutta).

Let us see how they come into existence and are used to launder the money.

The modus operandi:

XYZ Limited is a company which is listed, has operations in India and abroad and follows all the applicable corporate governance standards, secretarial standards and accounting standards. Its accounts are audited by best of the auditing firms and then analysed by a battalion of analysts from bankers to research companies. In short, the company needs to be transparent in all its transactions and procedures.

Then there are companies that are foreign multinationals which may or may not be listed in India but have the responsibility of reporting every single penny of money transparently to their Head Offices in foreign countries.

Both of these kinds of companies find themselves in soup when it comes to recording of certain expenses that cannot be shown in their financial statements in their true form.

These expenses are illicit payments required to pay off everyone, ranging from a local leader to a politician, from a dubious charitable trust to a famous political party, revenue official to a gangster, bureaucrat to a Naxalite commander or any other person demanding money while commanding authority to disapprove or disrupt the business of the company. Such under-hand payments also come handy in dispute resolutions and other amicable settlements. These payments need to be in cash or other forms of black money.

XYZ Limited, being one such company and confronting a similar problem (requirement of cash) writes a cheque of say INR 20 Mio (an amount equivalent to half of its daily revenue) to M/s ABC & Co., a partnership firm for availing their services related to payroll, temporary staff hiring and consultancy on staff appraisal systems. The payment is made vide cheque and tax is also deducted at source (TDS/ Withholding Tax) as per applicable rules so as to make this otherwise illegitimate transaction look legitimate.

The truth is that the payment made by XYZ Ltd. is a cover up transaction for the cash it has received from ABC. M/s ABC after it has received INR 20 Mio through cheque/wire transfer pays the full amount back in cash to M/s XYZ after deduction of commission for conversion of white money into black.

XYZ having got what it wanted to have, goes out of the picture. The story of black to white begins from here:

1. M/s ABC & Co. that got INR 20 Mio is a partnership firm which is controlled and managed by M/s Jockey & cartel.

2. First of all, ABC takes all steps to reduce the incidence of tax. It shows its income as a contractual income instead of commission (it will ask XYZ also to book it as contractual expense in its books of accounts) and then books various sub-contractual expenses to many other shell companies falling under the umbrella of Jockey's cartel. The possibility of ABC being a front company with a genuine business model and laundering money from behind (as discussed in Chapter – Bogus Business Companies) is not ruled out.

3. The money received by ABC from XYZ Ltd. of INR 20 Million is invested in form of equity share capital in a clutch of companies incorporated for the purpose. Say INR 5 Mio each is invested in 4 shell companies – D Pvt. Ltd., E Pvt. Ltd., F Pvt. Ltd., G Pvt. Ltd; all controlled by M/s Jockey & Cartel through layers of trusted or unaware and gullible people.

4. Thus, the Balance Sheets of D, E, F and G will look appear similar to the following:

D Private Limited

Liabilities	Amount (INR)	Assets	Amount (INR)
Equity Share Capital 500,000 shares of Face Value INR 10 each	5,000,000	Cash/ Loans and Advances/ Investments	5,000,000
Total	5,000,000	Total	5,000,000

5. Now Mr Darkhorse comes into the picture with say his INR 4 Million of black money which he wants to launder into white. He approaches Jockey, the

68

operator and controller of D Private Limited. Jockey shows some business entries in D which translate to loss demonstrating D as a loss making venture.

6. Various fictitious purchases, expenditures, write down of assets and bad debts etc. are shown so as to diminish the value of D Private Limited through losses.

7. Darkhorse therefore buys this company at a steep discount to its actual fair value. The entire shareholding in D Pvt. Ltd. is bought by Darkhorse and family. The shares of INR 10 each are bought by Darkhorse at INR 2 each. A valuation certificate from a Chartered Accountant friend is also arranged, if required valuing this company at steep discount due to its loss making future cash flows (discounted cash flow method).

8. Thus the official purchase consideration comes to INR 1 Million (500,000 x 2 = 1,000,000) for a company which can actually fetch INR 5 Million if its bank accounts, investments and other assets and the fictitious purchases and expenditures are reversed and realized to value. The parties to the transaction know this and therefore balance sale consideration of INR 4 Million is paid by Darkhorse to Jockey in black money.

9. Darkhorse, in effect gets full control over a company that has INR 5 Mio of money stashed in it by paying only INR 1 Mio. Money Laundered.

Remember the origin of D Private Limited is from sources which are completely white (received as contractual services to XYZ) and can be checked by anyone who cares to investigate. In the above case, we have used investment through equity share capital, where as the investment may be through loans as well as other instruments like preference shares, convertible debt etc. which we have covered in different chapters.

Further, the above example is extremely plain and simple for illustrating the conversion of black money into white. In real situations however, there will be a lot of layering while routing the money into the final company. Some of the challenges and standard features in such a modus operandi are as follows:

✓ There will be various layers through which investment will be routed from M/s ABC & Co. to D Private Limited. The shell corporation – D Private Limited will be held by various shell corporations in between. The intermediary firms or companies will have complex shareholding structure. There could be a holding company structure in between, whereby there will be a holding company controlling the movement of money in series of transactions between various interlocked and networked companies.

- ✓ The money gets routed into D Private Limited through a maze of similar transactions going in and out of the company.
- ✓ D Private Limited has its directors as personal servants, drivers, cooks, security guards, maids etc. of Jockey's trusted lieutenants and even the relatives of such people living in far flung areas. These people are uneducated and untraceable most of the times.
- ✓ The address of D Pvt. Ltd. is on the outskirts of a city or it may be completely fake. The address changes when the operator gets to know that some investigation is going about the company. The trick of the game is to make the puzzle hugely complicated for the investigators so that they either drop the case or settle it for some paltry amount.
- ✓ Different layers created for routing money are made more complicated by incorporating companies in different regions and different states so that if a part of it gets caught by a Tax Officer of a particular area, the other part of the network remains out of his jurisdiction.
- ✓ The investigations hit the wall when the money gets routed through offshore shell corporations located in tax havens where the detail of such companies including their controllers is only a mystery.
- ✓ Further, please note that offshore shell corporations can be in form of offshore trusts also.

After explaining the above method, let me tell you that Finance Bill 2017 has given a huge blow to this method by stating that if the sale amount for transfer of unquoted share of a company is less than the Fair Market Value (FMV) of such share, the FMV of such share will be taken as sale amount and taxed accordingly. Moreover, if any professional – Chartered Accountant, Merchant Banker or Valuer gives incorrect information in his report or certificate then such professional will be liable for penalty.

Thus, if The Income Tax Department could find out that the purchases and other expenditures and losses of D Private Limited are fictitious, then they may charge tax on Whitehorse (the seller of D Pvt. Ltd.)

Moreover, if there is any accumulated loss in D Pvt. Ltd then such loss will also not be allowed to be carried forward for further tax benefit in future years when the shareholding of the company is transferred from Whitehorse to Darkhorse unless and until D Pvt. Ltd. is a small company with turnover not exceeding INR 250 Million and eligible as a start-up i.e. incorporated between 01/Apr/2016 and 31/Mar/2019. Thus, the government has tried to reduce this method's abuse to a large extent.

POINTS TO PONDER:

It may be noted that shell corporations are not just those explained in this chapter but even those entities that conduct bogus businesses as explained in Method 11 are shell entities.

Question: If shell corporations are so dangerously used in money laundering activities, why they cannot be banned by one and all jurisdictions?

Answer: Banning is not a solution to everything that is misused. Shell corporations are a type of Special Purpose Companies (SPCs) that are essential for bona fide business purposes like ring fencing of assets, raising funds, effective and better management of assets with different owners, facilitating mergers & acquisitions and demergers, facilitating investments in on-shore and off-shore projects etc. Any company that is incorporated for a specific purpose will at first be a shell corporation only. If shell corporations are banned, the launderers will form a full-fledged business company in a tax haven and use it for routing the money.

The government has initiated various measures to curb the misuse of shell companies and now there is a more coordinated action by all the investigative agencies domestically as well as across the globe towards the common purpose of unearthing black money.

Method 12.2: Offshore Shell Companies:

Offshore shell corporations are the mainstay of Money Laundering schemes. They are corporations/trusts/ joint ventures/ firms etc. incorporated outside the jurisdiction of home country (say India) and not for the purpose of doing any genuine business activity but for routing of money from one place to another.

These companies are generally incorporated in countries where the tax is either nil or minimal, Anti-Money Laundering procedures either do not exist or exist only for compliance on paper and the available banking systems have the potential to wire transfer any amount of money anywhere in the world through correspondent banking arrangements. Many global banks even have their full-fledged branches in these countries.

Use of offshore shell companies is not always illegal, but sometimes it takes advantage of loopholes in tax laws and tax treaties between the countries.

There can be completely genuine offshore structures. For example: If tax in Luxembourg is nil/minimal, billing and sales booking can be done in the Head Office of the company which is incorporated in Luxembourg. Similarly a holding company can be incorporated there which will take all the dividends from offshore subsidiaries that do not have any dividend distribution tax.

Then there can be some dubious structures too. For example: If someone wants to buy a house in Spain, he will have to shell out extra 10% of the cost as Land Transfer Tax (LTT) but this tax is not payable if he does not buys the house himself and buys the shares of the company that owns the house (we will discuss this in detail in chapter on evasion of stamp duty tax).

Similarly, if there is no tax on profits and Capital Gains in a particular country, it makes business sense if the investments in India are being routed through a Shell Holding company located in that country.

The question that is significant is from where that holding company has got its money? If the answer is through Trade Based Money Laundering (TBML) or Informal Remittance System i.e. through Hawala then this is the illegal part.

There are many jurisdictions in the mainstream UK, USA and Europe which fall in the category of tax havens since they want to attract investments by providing tax benefits but then colour of the money is the same and so it's hard to distinguish between the good and the bad tax havens.

Sewn with sophisticated Money Laundering techniques, offshore shell companies and tax havens have respected names for themselves; they are now better known as International Business Corporations (IBCs) and Offshore Financial Centres (OFCs) respectively.

Some of the countries that are widely regarded as OFCs are as follows:

Alderney	Andorra	Anguilla	Antigua
Aruba	Austria	Bahamas	Barbados
Belize	Bermuda	British Virgin Islands	Cayman Islands
Cook Islands	Costa Rica	Cyprus	Delaware (USA)
Dubai	Dutch Antilles	Gibraltar	Guernsey
Hong Kong	Hungary	Ireland (Dublin)	Isle Of Man
Jersey	Labuan	Lebanon	Liberia
Liechtenstein	Luxembourg	Macao	Madeira
Malta	Marianas	Marshall Islands	Mauritius
Monaco	Montserrat	Nauru	Nevada (USA)

Niue	Panama	Saint Kitts	Nevis
Saint Lucia	Saint Pierre et Miquelon	Saint Vincent and the Grenadines	Samoa
Sark	Seychelles	Singapore	Switzerland
Turks and Caicos Islands	Vanuatu	United Kingdom	Wyoming (USA)

It is no coincidence that some of the tax havens are same locations which once served as bases for sea pirates. Pirates went to these places as they were located near to prominent commercial centres but had different jurisdiction. Money Launderers go to these places for the same reasons.

The list of 56 jurisdictions given above is not exhaustive, the total is believed at somewhere around 70. Here, the money flows from one place to another depending upon the comparative advantage of relevant jurisdictions. IBCs/offshore shell companies in these jurisdictions are formed with minimal formalities, either with or without partnering with a local person there.

There are accountants, attorneys and other professionals who specialise in creation of IBCs in OFCs and charge only few dollars annually for the maintenance and compliance formalities. There is a very simple reason why these professionals as well as countries/OFCs exist and flourish facilitating creation of IBCs. It's the money. The professionals need money and so do OFCs and even banks. If a Russian with his unaccounted wealth comes to me for buying some estate in my island; should I do this much needed business transaction with him or turn him off to some other island by asking his source of money. This leads to the whole problem and the quantum of the problem can be gauged from the fact that information leak from a single law firm's office from a single OFC – 'Panama' led to:

✓ Resignation of Prime Minister of Iceland
✓ Censors in China blocking everything related to Panama Papers on the internet
✓ President of Russia fuming about a western conspiracy to defame him
✓ President of Ukraine and many other politicians being questioned for being clients list of this law firm
✓ Prime Minister of Britain experiencing worst week of his premiership due to his late father's connections with the firm
✓ Demonstrations in Argentina
✓ War in Azerbaijan

✓ Investigations in approximately 80 countries leading to many more events and disclosures.

The Great Panama Leak (in brief)

Panama Islands are located across Panama Canal between North America and South America. The islands and Panama City has a population of ~2.5 Million people but it is a big name in tax havens list for long now. US Dollar is accepted as a currency there.

In April and May, 2016 two journalists namely Bastian Obermayer and Frederik Obermaier of Germany, working for a newspaper Suddeutsche Zeitung gave to the world an entire database of a major Panamanian law firm specialising in setting up of anonymous IBCs.

The law firm's name was Mossack Fonseca (Mosfon) and the data was provided to the journalists by some insider who did not reveal his true identity and called himself John Doe. The journalists gave a name to this data leak – The Panama Papers.

This data leak was an astounding act of bravery with a size at 2.6 TB (Terabytes) containing 11.5 Million documents that included records of more than 200,000 offshore shell companies. Mosfon had its Head Office in Panama and its branches in Jersey and Isle of Man with a solid network of intermediaries including attorneys, accountants and even banks.

What ensued after Panama Leak was anarchy in the global financial world with more than 400 journalists working on these Panama Papers and the names emanating from these papers sparing no major country in the world. Political leaders (including presidents and prime ministers), bureaucrats, businessmen, sportsmen, sports associations and other celebrities from across the globe have been named in these papers.

The problem which Panama leak offers to investigators is that while the shell companies are registered in Panama, the bank accounts of these companies is located in many other countries.

India connection: Names of hundreds of Indians having offshore shell corporate connection with Panama have been revealed in the papers. Investigations are under process.

Some of the interesting aspects of offshore shell companies are as follows:

Bearer Shares:

Offshore shell companies or IBCs are Bearer Share Corporations meaning thereby that if you misplace the shares of the company who actually misplace and loose the company.

These share certificates are like the currency notes. Whosoever holds them owns them. There are jurisdictions as stated above, where companies are legally owned through the bearer shares.

Benefit: Complete privacy/anonymity. There is no requirement of a public share register, no shareholder disclosure and no beneficial ownership disclosure. They are transferable through agreement (no format prescribed) as well as through physical handover and the transfer can be anywhere in the world without any registration.

The details of these shareholdings/ ownership are however immaculately maintained by the law firms who deal in creation of such corporations and if someone looses these shares can get them re-issued by giving a letter of indemnity in favour of such law firms provided no one else gets his hands over such shares in which case the company is lost.

Numbered Accounts:

'He has got huge money in his secret Swiss bank account', we have often heard similar statements lot many times. The secret bank account being talked about here is a numbered account which means the owner of the account is not a person but a number. Every accountholder who opens such account with the bank is assigned a number (say a pass code) and that number becomes the identity of account's owner. Even the systems and the staff of such banks know the accountholder not by his name but by his number. Anyone who knows that number can operate the bank account, much like bearer shares.

Benefit: No tax official knows that how many numbers are known by Mr Darkhorse. The pass codes could have been stored anywhere or may be nowhere if he has memorised them.

The banking secrecy laws of many jurisdictions give banks the power not to disclose anything related to identity of their accountholders.

The reason for their existence is the same - Money. If there is demand from people for such an account, for such a service, it is provided because it means business.

Want even more anonymity! You get it!

There are various international agencies operating from nowhere and everywhere who provide fake identity documents for all the countries listed therein. A simple search on the internet and many such service providers appear on your screen. It may be noted that many of them will just appear once and never again when searched from the same IP (Internet Protocol Address of your machine). Some of them require downloading of browsers like 'Onion' famous for anonymous routing and only then a user will be able to view and transact.

Many such service providers guarantee that these real looking fake documents will be issued only after registering all the data in government's repository. For example: if you obtain a (real) fake passport from them, then any officer in immigration checking that passport would be easily able to verify the details from issuing government's database.

All this goes well for the money launderers who need it only for compliance of KYC norms and that too relaxed ones.

Next thing launderers want is a fancy address that remains open *at least on paper*. For that, there are multitudes of companies especially in OFCs which specialise in servicing the offshore shell companies and provide mail drop facilities. They can even arrange nominee directors as well as local partners for such companies. Now days it is easy to redirect phone and fax lines to any number in this world and therefore Darkhorse, can attend to a call made to his office number in Hong Kong while sitting in India through call forwarding managed by specialised companies.

Moreover, one should not be surprised to hear that in many jurisdictions, it is possible to buy a prepaid phone number by just paying cash. No ID/Address proof is required. Such a phone number is as good as an anonymous one. People use it, throw it and then take a new one for new conversation.

Next is the use of **Shelf Companies.** In many OFCs, it is possible to buy a Shell Company which has a track record and an originally invested share capital. These are shelf companies allowing their buyers to buy them across the shelf.

Shelf companies are second-hand shell companies. The law firms specialising in IBCs set up these companies and keep them in reserve so that they can be sold to clients who need a Shell Company that does not look as if it has just been established.

OFCs and IBCs are used to stash wealth abroad that can be transmitted to/ from India through various means like Over-Invoicing and Under-Invoicing in international trade (as discussed in detail in chapter on TBML), Loans by IBCs to Indian Companies, Sale/ Purchase of Assets located in India by IBCs, Investments in Indian Companies and Participatory Notes etc.

It is important to briefly discuss about **Participatory Notes** here.

Participatory Notes commonly referred to as P-Notes or PNs are financial instruments through which individual foreign investors or hedge funds who do not want to disclose their identity can invest in Indian markets anonymously.

Registered Foreign Institutional Investors (FIIs), foreign banks and brokerage companies based in India issue P-Notes to foreign investors and invest in Indian stock market on their behalf. Any dividends or Capital Gains collected from the underlying securities go back to the investors through such FIIs.

While a common investor has to fill up KYC forms, provide PAN number and proof of address, a P-Note investor can simply keep his investment anonymous. This route was intended to attract foreign investment in India by making it easier for foreign investors to invest. However, it created a 'legal' way to route unaccounted wealth in Indian equities, encouraging the black money monster.

The wealth stashed overseas, when it does not comes to India is used abroad by black money holders for various purposes like:

✓ Living abroad most of the time.
✓ Marriage of children and other celebrations overseas.
✓ Funding of children's overseas education and their living expenses.
✓ Acquisition of property overseas etc.

POINTS TO PONDER:

$ It may be noted that Securities and Exchange Board of India (SEBI) has now made it mandatory for the P-Notes holders to adhere to Indian Know your customer (KYC) norms. SEBI has also put curbs on the transferability of P-notes between two foreign investors and has increased the frequency of reporting by P-notes issuers.

$ Government of India aware of the use of offshore jurisdictions is set to revise many tax treaties to take off the advantage available to companies investing there from.

$ International pressure is mounting on OFCs, IBCs and Banks dealing with them to follow Anti-Money Laundering procedures.

$ Government of India has stipulated various measures in the International Taxation arena like General Anti-Avoidance Measures (GAAR), rules on Place of Effective Management (POEM) and Base Erosion in Profit Shifting (BEPS), Auto-Exchange of Tax Information between countries, Amendments in Tax Treaties with Tax Havens and many more; all of which give precedence to substance over form and are aimed at tax avoidance and money laundering through abuse of various loopholes. Government of today has the power to disregard any structure and any modus-operandi that has been created to avoid tax and/or smells of money laundering. It has powers vide enough within Taxation law, Foreign Exchange Law, Benami Property Law and Black Money Law to confiscate all the Dirty Money of a Black Money holder.

METHOD 13

Penny Stocks

This method details how Money laundering is done by manipulating stock markets.

It should be no surprise to the stock market brokers, analysts and investors that many times the prices of stocks are found to be rigged and especially when it comes to Penny Stocks.

Penny Stocks refer to shares that are listed on a Stock Exchange and are trading at extremely small prices. They are called Penny Stocks because they are available at the price of a penny. Although there cannot be any single threshold amount for classification of Penny Stocks, the ballpark price can range from zero to INR 20/-. I say zero (0) because they can be trading at even fraction of a rupee. In US and Europe, their price may be up to $5 and £5 respectively.

Penny stocks are also known as 'cent stocks' in some countries. The market capitalisation of these stocks is also low – may be a few hundred million INR in Indian markets or up to ~USD 250 Mio in US bourses.

These shares are usually of companies in which traders and investors are not much interested. Penny companies may or may not be having any significant business and it won't be any surprise if they turn out to be shell or bogus companies.

Modus Operandi 1: Use of Penny Stocks for Money Laundering

A company – Tar Oils Limited was once a small oil refinery but now it is either non-operative or the promoters lack interest in its business. The company generally posts losses or negligible profits. Its operations have stalled. No one knows anything about its assets except the book value available in the Stock Exchange filings. Its share price hovers around INR 2/- per share.

PS: There are no rules of selecting a particular kind of a Penny Stock for the purposes of Money Laundering. Any Penny Stock that has low trading volume and whose stock price can be manipulated easily with or without the connivance of its promoters is selected by the money launderers. Let's say Tar Oils Limited gets selected for the purpose.

Participants in the scheme:

1. Mr Darkhorse – a black money holder. He has INR 1 Million of black money and wants to convert this black money into white money.

2. M/s Jockey & Co. – an entry operator. He is a lesser known stock broker but is popular for his ingenuity. He secretly earns good amount of money from helping his clients convert their black money into white. In this illicit business, he is helped by many of his stock broker friends and even some promoters and/ or managers (insiders) of few Penny Stock companies. They form a cartel to rig the share prices.

Darkhorse searches for a stock broker who has experience in Money Laundering. He finds Jockey and the game begins.

Jockey asks Darkhorse to buy 300,000 shares of Tar Oils Limited (Tar Oils) at the prevailing market price of say INR 2/-.

Darkhorse thus spends INR 600,000/- of his white money and buys 300,000 shares of Tar Oils.

He simultaneously hands over his black money of INR 1 Million to Mr Jockey which he wants back at a later date in form of white money. Jockey and his cartel of stock brokers smurf this amount in their bank accounts.

Next step is Circular Trading. The brokers trade the shares of Tar Oils among themselves in such a manner that the price of the stock is artificially increased.

The concept of Circular Trading is explained as follows:

Circular Trading is a manipulative trading strategy where buy or sell orders are entered into by a trader with full knowledge that an exactly off-setting counter offer will be entered by some other trader or traders at roughly the same time. These persons know each other, work as a cartel and split the order size among them.

They buy and sell high volume of shares among themselves with an understanding of either increasing or decreasing the share price at specified intervals.

If they want to increase the price, they will buy and sell the scrip at continuously increasing/ higher prices which will take the scrip price higher and higher. In this, the sell or ask bid will come first at a higher price and then the buy bid will be submitted to match the sell price. The volumes of off-setting bids will match each other and the trades in this manner will take the price of the scrip up.

Similarly, if the cartel wants to decrease the price, exactly opposite will be done.

Circular Trading is a complete price rigging technique. It works well in case of Penny Stocks as the actual volumes are completely dried up and the price can be easily manipulated up or down to any desired level. Let us take an example:

M/s Jockey & Co.'s cartel comprises 10 brokers namely Aluwalia (A), Banarasi (B), Chetan (C), Deepak (D), Eshaan (E), Farhaan (F), Gaurav (G), Harshad (H), Isha (I) and Jockey (J).

Now to manipulate or artificially inflate the price of Tar Oils; J sells 30,000 shares of Tar Oils to A at INR 2.25/- per share. (To reduce suspicion, J will place a bid to sell 30,000 shares at INR 2.50 first but since there will be no buyer, he will then gradually reduce his bid to INR 2.25/- per share to which A will respond and buy the shares.)

B will buy say 50,000 shares at INR 2.5/- per share from D in a separate transaction.

A too will find a buyer in

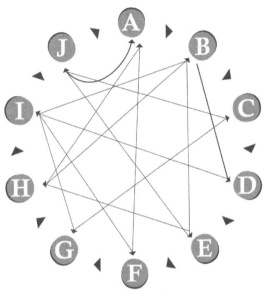

A Web Of Criss-Cross Transactions Between Brokers

F for offloading his 30,000 shares at INR 3/- per share.

Likewise, the trading continues for days, months and even years in a criss-cross fashion and the trading volume as well as the price of Tar Oils will slowly move up:

The financing for these trades may come either from legitimate sources or from black money received from people like Darkhorse.

Circular Trading is also touted as "Pump and Dump" scheme globally.

Over a period, the volumes of Tar Oils get pumped up from a few hundred shares to a few hundred thousand shares in a single transaction before the shares are finally dumped upon some innocent gullible investors.

To avoid any direct attention, there are pre-planned intervals when the share price will be made to go down in between but the net change is always an increase.

While these transactions continue, Jockey also shakes hand with promoters and other insiders of Tar Oils Limited. They do a bit of hard work and release some big positive news about the company such as:

✓ The company is in talks of being acquired by a big company,

✓ The company has got a big sales order,

✓ The land bank and other assets of the company are steeply under-priced,

✓ The management has recently got restructured etc.

All such news is dumped in the media including social media. The crooks, we know are efficient in the use of Facebook, Twitter, WhatsApp etc. for all wrong reasons. They also circulate this news in the stock broking circles with full vigour. After all, the value of promoters' stake in the company will also increase and they can then offload some of their shares to the unaware gullible investor who gets attracted to buy Tar Oil shares.

As the brokers are simultaneously working on increasing the share price of Tar Oils behind the scenes through Circular Trading; the credibility of such news also gets justified which in turn justifies the logic of share price increase.

Remember M/s Jockey & Co. is fully capable to increase the price of Tar Oils by Circular Trading without any support from the company's side which is only additional.

The combined effect of these actions by Jockey and his cartel as well as those of company's insiders is that the price of Tar Oils reaches INR 5.50/-. This increase of 1.75x (175%) is considered on conservative basis. In reality, even a 10 times increase in price of a Penny Stock is too small to raise eyebrows.

It is at this point that M/s Jockey & Co. calls upon Darkhorse to offload (sell) his 300,000 shares of Tar Oils. Darkhorse sells his shares and Jockey along with his cartel eagerly buys these shares in the ratio in which they had made profits from the Circular Trading of stock and all this happens on a Stock Exchange. Darkhorse places a selling bid at INR 5.50/- and Jockey and his friends readily agree to buy these shares at this artificial price.

The outcome:

Darkhorse gets to show that he made a great stock selection in form of Tar Oils and made a sweet Capital Gain Profit of INR 1.05 Million (300,000 shares x (Selling Price @ INR 5.50 – Buying Price @ INR 2.00 = Profit @ INR 3.50 per share). Black Money given and Capital Gain received. Money Laundered.

A commission @ 2–5% of the transaction value would also have been paid to Jockey under the table.

At the end, Jockey and his cartel are left with 300,000 shares of Tar Oils. They can sell these shares to any outsider who is interested in buying them at any price as their real motive has already been achieved and black money received along with commission.

Tax Free Money Laundering:

The whole process mentioned above may take anywhere from few months to few years depending upon the safety and caution exercised by the parties.

If Darkhorse has held the shares for more than one year before selling them over Stock Exchange, it amounts to Long Term Capital Gain (LTCG) which is tax free under Indian Income Tax Act 1961. Thus results in tax free Money Laundering.

Otherwise if, Darkhorse is in a hurry, he shall ask Jockey to complete the whole transaction within few months and book the gain as Short Term Capital Gain (STCG) which is taxable.

Please note that in real scenarios, Darkhorse will try to appear clever by doing various other stock trades in his account during the same time period as that of aforesaid transaction so as to disguise Tar Oils Trade as just one of his many trades.

Conclusion:

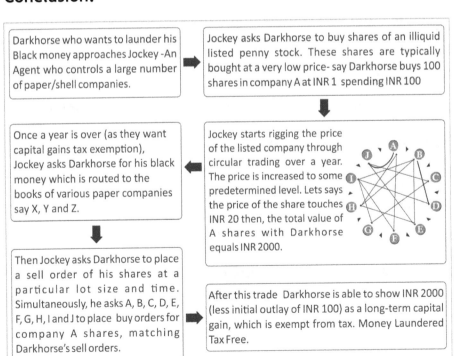

Darkhorse who wants to launder his Black money approaches Jockey -An Agent who controls a large number of paper/shell companies.

Jockey asks Darkhorse to buy shares of an illiquid listed penny stock. These shares are typically bought at a very low price- say Darkhorse buys 100 shares in company A at INR 1 spending INR 100

Once a year is over (as they want capital gains tax exemption), Jockey asks Darkhorse for his black money which is routed to the books of various paper companies say X, Y and Z.

Jockey starts rigging the price of the listed company through circular trading over a year. The price is increased to some predetermined level. Lets says the price of the share touches INR 20 then, the total value of A shares with Darkhorse equals INR 2000.

Then Jockey asks Darkhorse to place a sell order of his shares at a particular lot size and time. Simultaneously, he asks A, B, C, D, E, F, G, H, I and J to place buy orders for company A shares, matching Darkhorse's sell orders.

After this trade Darkhorse is able to show INR 2000 (less initial outlay of INR 100) as a long-term capital gain, which is exempt from tax. Money Laundered Tax Free.

In this scheme, black money may go to Jockey either at the start of the scheme or on its completion, depending upon the terms between the parties.

Modus Operandi 2: Penny Stocks as a means of Tax Evasion:

Similar to their use in laundering money, Penny Stocks are also used as means for manufacturing fictitious profits and losses. How? Let's take a look at the following scheme. The first stage is same as stated in previous modus operandi:

Participants in the scheme (1 Added):

1. Mr Darkhorse – a black money holder. He has INR 1 Million of black money and wants to convert this black money into white money.

2. M/s Jockey & Co. – an entry operator. He is a lesser known stock broker but is popular for his ingenuity. He secretly earns good amount of money from helping his clients convert their black money into white. In this illicit business, he is helped by many of his stock broker friends and even some promoters and/ or managers (insiders) of few Penny Stock companies. They form a cartel to rig the share prices.

3. Mr Whitehorse – a businessman who wants to incur some fictitious losses on paper so as to avoid or reduce his Income Tax on some real stock market gains i.e. he is willing to incur INR 1 Million of loss in white money.

Darkhorse searches for a stock broker who has experience in Money Laundering. He finds Jockey and the game begins.

Jockey asks Mr Darkhorse to buy 300,000 shares of Tar Oils Limited (Tar Oils) at the prevailing market price of say INR 2/-. Darkhorse thus spends INR 600,000/- of his white money and buys 300,000 shares of Tar Oils.

He simultaneously hands over his black money of INR 1 Million to Mr Jockey which he wants back at a later date in form of white money. Jockey and his cartel of stock brokers smurf this amount in their bank accounts.

Next step is Circular Trading and the combined effect of actions by M/s Jockey & Co. and company's insiders is that the price of Tar Oils reaches INR 5.50/-.

At this stage, Jockey calls upon Darkhorse to offload (sell) his 300,000 shares of Tar Oils at INR 5.50/- per share.

(Up to here, the story remained same. Now a small twist is introduced)

Here M/s Jockey & Co. has another special client in the name of Whitehorse who wants to incur some loss on paper. Therefore, when Jockey along with his cartel places the selling bid on behalf of Darkhorse for selling 300,000 shares @ INR 5.50 each, he at the exactly same time, places a buying bid on behalf of Whitehorse for the same number of shares. Whitehorse buys the shares from Darkhorse and pays in white money. Darkhorse gains INR 1.05 Mio and his black money gets laundered. He moves away after paying commission to Jockey.

Whitehorse gets 300,000 Tar Oils Limited (TOL) shares bought @ INR 5.50 each, the actual price of which is INR 2 per share if we negate the effect of Circular Trading. Thus, the price of TOL is bound to fall to its original price of INR 2/- once M/s Jockey & Co. is out of company's trading and these share are 'dumped' in the market. In such case, Whitehorse suffers a loss of INR 1.05 Mio (300,000 shares x (Buying Price @ INR 5.50 – Selling Price @ INR 2.00 = Loss @ INR 3.50 per share). However, he is compensated by Jockey with an equal amount in black money (less his commission). This is the black money that Darkhorse gave to him.

Whitehorse moves away after taking a loss entry in his books of accounts. Purposes served.

In reality, Whitehorse shall decide upon the quantum of loss to be incurred by selling at various levels i.e. executing the transaction in piecemeal instead of a lump sum. Further, Jockey shall involve some other broker in punching of off-setting bids so as to avoid suspicion. *(We will see this nexus in detail in our F&O chapter).*

The whole modus operandi mentioned here may take anywhere from few months to few years, depending upon the safety and caution exercised by the parties. The parties manufacture a Short Term Transaction (giving rise to STCG and Loss) or a Long Term Transaction (giving rise to LTCG or Loss) depending upon their requirements.

Why Penny Stocks?

The reason why listed Penny Stocks are selected for the above schemes is as under:

- $ **Avoids Attention:** Investors, Traders and other market participants generally tend to ignore Penny Stocks and their price movements. The markets focus more on blue chip stocks rather than Penny Stocks.
- $ **Easy to Manipulate:** Because of their low price and low trading volumes, it is easy to manipulate the stock price of Penny Stocks. The promoters of many such companies also lack trust.
- $ **Genuineness:** The sale/ purchase transactions carried out through Stock Exchange appear to be fair, transparent and genuine to public at large.

$ **Tax Benefit:** Generally no tax is payable if there is LTCG on purchase and sale of securities through Stock Exchange. The rate of tax on LTCG is also low and the definition of Long Term Period is just one year.

$ **Less Scope of Complaint:** Mostly complaints are made to stock exchanges and/or SEBI (the stock market regulator) when someone looses in the stock market but feels cheated by the ingenuity of other party. However, in the schemes mentioned above, both buying as well as selling parties work under collusion and so the losing party will not feel cheated.

POINTS TO PONDER:

$ According to an Income Tax Department investigation, they uncovered a trail of INR 38,000 crores (~USD 6 Billion) involving manipulation in 84-Bombay Stock Exchange (BSE)-listed penny stocks through ~5,000 listed and unlisted firms, many of which were shell companies.
(Source: Hindustan Times, New Delhi 22-Nov-2016)

$ It is not just penny stocks but brokers &/or investors have been found rigging the price of well known companies too by using technologies like Algorithmic or High Frequency Trading where users of these techniques enjoy relative advantage over others and to avoid attention, the cartel's traders may be based in distant locations.

$ The government is contemplating to take off benefits and privileges enjoyed by penny stocks including imposition of higher rate of tax on LTCG from stocks. Many penny stocks have already been compulsorily delisted by Stock Exchanges.

$ Income Tax Department is always free to question the intention of stock brokers and their clients behind investing large sums of money in companies that have no significant business models.

$ Circular Trading is illegal and if found guilty, the licenses of such stock brokers could be revoked.

METHOD 14

Fake Contract Notes

This method comes to picture when Mr Darkhorse is in tremendous hurry to launder funds and that too without tax.

The solution is kept ready in form of a Penny Stock by Mr Jockey. The solution is although simple but costly as well as risky.

Jockey and Darkhorse strike a deal whereby Jockey sells shares in a Penny Stock to Darkhorse for a small amount. *The catch being that Jockey does a little forgery here and issues a fake back dated contract note.* The contract note will bear date of at least 12 months back (so to avoid Capital Gains tax on the LTCG). In the interim, Jockey and his cartel has already moved up the price of this share using Circular Trading as discussed in Penny Stocks method. Darkhorse then sells the Penny Stock back to Jockey and his team at a higher price booking a LTCG in a very short span of time. Darkhorse hands over an equivalent amount in black money to Jockey. Money Laundered tax free.

In case, there is no Penny Stock ready for this purpose in the armour of Jockey, he will take the black money from Darkhorse in advance and use Circular Trading to inflate the price of a Penny Stock with this black money.

Say a Penny Stock, Tar Oils Limited (TOL) is selected for the purpose. Jockey shall issue a contract note that shows sale of TOL to Darkhorse at its actual low price but the date is forged to at least 12 months back. Jockey and his cartel increase the price of TOL by Circular Trading to a predetermined level at which Darkhorse sells the stock booking a LTCG in a short span of time. Money Laundered tax free.

MODUS OPERANDI

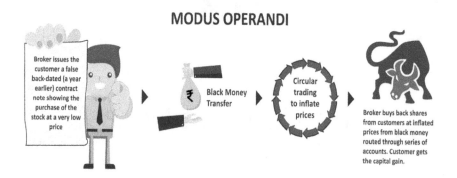

The brokers engaged in the field of Money Laundering and evading taxes are professional enough to continuously rig the prices of some Penny Stocks and keep them in their inventory ready for sale.

POINTS TO PONDER:

$ The method is fraught with risks as it involves forgery of date of buy leg of this transaction whereas the dematerialised account statements and details of transaction from stock exchange will easily reveal the actual date.

$ Although proving legally that this scheme has been used for laundering money may be difficult but Tax Officers are well aware of this modus operandi and certainly ask the rationale behind investing in a penny stock which has no good business.

METHOD 15

Sale and Buy-Back of Physical Shares

A s a rule, all the fresh issuances of the shares need to be in DEMAT form only. Thus, holding of shares in physical form is an outdated phenomenon now but certain investors may still be holding some shares in physical form.

According to extant guidelines, a person who holds some shares in physical form can continue holding them in physical form but he will have to get them dematerialised in case he wants to trade/sell them over a Stock Exchange.

Dematerialisation is a process by which Physical Share Certificates of an investor are converted to an equal number of shares in electronic form and credited to his DEMAT Account opened with a Depository Participant (DP) who in turn maintains an account with a Depository company. This process makes the holding of shares more safe, secure and transparent.

Physical Share Certificates can be converted into dematerialised form anytime by surrendering them to a DP who will credit equal number of shares in the account of the owner.

Those who are interested in buying and selling of the shares in physical form will enter into a sale-purchase transaction through a Sale Purchase Agreement. A Transfer Deed will be also be executed where a transfer stamp is affixed and the documents are then sent to the company (or its share transfer agents, if any) for registration.

Let us now see how Physical Share Certificates are used as means to launder funds.

The modus operandi:

Participants in the scheme:

1. Mr Darkhorse – a black money holder. He has INR 1 Million of black money and wants to convert this black money into white money.

2. M/s Jockey & Co. – an entry operator. He is a lesser known stock broker but is popular for his ingenuity. He secretly earns good amount of money from helping his clients convert their black money into white. In this illicit business, he is helped by many of his stock broker friends and even some promoters and/ or managers (insiders) of few Penny Stock companies. Many times they form a cartel to rig the share prices through Circular Trading.

Darkhorse searches for a stock broker who has experience in Money Laundering activities. He finds Jockey and the game begins.

Mr Jockey has in his armour, few very old Physical Share Certificates of TOL; (a Penny Stock company) registered in his name or in the name of his trusted lieutenants.

He sells these shares to Darkhorse at their current prevailing price which is reasonably very low and takes over his millions of black money at the same time. *The catch here is that the transfer deed and the agreement through which this sale-purchase transaction is being executed is dated back by at least one year.*

As the legal validity of a transfer deed is for one year, it allows the back dating of this transaction. Secondly, collusion of TOL's management with M/s Jockey & Co. makes it possible to get this back dated transfer deed registered with the company.

In the interim, the black money received by M/s Jockey & Co. is smurfed into his various bank accounts and the price of TOL is inflated artificially to some predetermined level through Circular Trading method as discussed in the chapter on Penny Stocks.

After the back dated transfer deed gets registered with the company, Jockey helps Darkhorse get these shares dematerialised in his name. Thus, Darkhorse becomes the owner of these shares in DEMAT form and can trade in them through stock exchanges.

Now he sells these shares back to M/s Jockey and Co. at the inflated pre-decided price thereby making legitimate Capital Gains in his books of accounts. Money Laundered.

MODUS OPERANDI

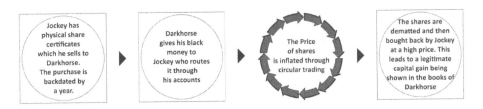

In effect, the black money received from Darkhorse was routed back to him through tax free Capital Gains.

If in case, Mr Darkhorse is willing to pay taxes on his laundered black money, he need not dematerialise the shares. He can sell these shares back to Jockey in the physical form through a Transfer Deed in the same manner in which he bought them except that now the transfer deed will bear the actual date. In such case, he will have to pay tax on his Capital Gain since the transaction did not occur through a Stock Exchange.

POINTS TO PONDER:

$ This modus operandi is dying a slow death as the physical share certificates are getting extinct. Moreover, the Finance Bill of 2017 has laid that if Securities Transaction Tax has not been paid at the time of purchase of shares (i.e. purchase of shares was not done through stock exchanges), then the long term capital gain on sale of such shares will not be exempt from tax. Thus, long term capital gains where physical shares were purchased will be taxable dealing a huge blow to the above method.

$ Further the government is tightening its grip on Penny Stocks with each passing day.

METHOD 16-A

Derivative Trading — Futures & Options (F&O) Segment

Part-1

After discussing modus operandi in Penny Stock Market, I would also like to touch upon another facet of Stock Exchange Market where manipulation is done for Money Laundering purposes. The segment is F&O segment and the method is Derivative Trading.

F&O are traded for various underlying, be it stocks, currency or commodities. Manipulation is possible in all of them. For laundering of black money, any underlying asset which is easy to manipulate at a given point of time is selected for the purpose.

In the earlier chapters, we had seen how brokers/ entry operators connived with each other to manipulate the price of small shares while facilitating laundering of black money into white. In this chapter, we will see how F&O segment is used as a tool by the same brokers in making the Money Laundering process more complex and effective than the schemes discussed earlier.

Besides Money Laundering, F&O segment is also used to evade taxes. Here, a broker either by himself or through his nexus with other brokers forms a cartel to generate profits as well as losses for his clients. The profit goes to those who want to convert their black money into white or those who want to show fancy numbers to their investors and the losses are kept by those who want to reduce their profits to evade Income Tax.

With the advent of mobile banking and swift trading applications (apps) present on every trader's mobile phone, executing such illicit schemes has become faster and easier than before.

Before proceeding towards the modus operandi used in Money Laundering through F&O segment, let us revisit some of the important concepts used in the trade:

Futures Contract:

A futures contract (commonly known as futures) is a contract between two parties to buy or sell an asset at a certain time in future at a certain price.

The price (also known as the futures price), time to settlement and other terms which are usually standardized are agreed upon in advance on the transaction date. Futures price can be higher or lower than the spot price prevailing in the cash segment.

Example:

We are in January and you enter into a futures contract to purchase 100 shares of XYZ stock at INR 50 a share on April 1. It means you have got 100 shares in XYZ futures and the contract price is INR 5,000 (100 x 50). If the Market Value of the stock goes up before April 1, you can sell the contract early for a profit. Let's say the price of XYZ stock rises to INR 52 a share on March 1. If you sell your futures for 100 shares, you will fetch a price of INR 5,200, and make a profit of INR 200. Similarly, if it goes below INR 50, it will be a loss for you.

The same goes for going short i.e. if you enter into a futures contract to sell 100 shares of XYZ stock at INR 50 a share on April 1. You have sold 100 shares in XYZ futures and the contract price is again INR 5,000 which you have received on the sale in this case. If XYZ stock drops to INR 48 a share on March 1, you pay only INR 4,800 and make a profit of INR 200 but if it goes above INR 50, it will mean a loss to you as you will have to pay more to buy and cover your short sell position.

Options Contract:

Options contracts are mainly of two types:

1.   Call Options
2.   Put Options

Call Option:

A call option gives the holder the **right to buy** an asset by a certain date for a certain price. Call options are purchased by traders who think the price of the asset will go up. Similarly, call options are sold by traders who think the price of the asset will go down.

When you buy a call option, you are buying the right to buy an asset at a strike price also known as exercise price, regardless of what the price of that asset may be in future. As a call option buyer, you will exercise this option only when the price in the market (spot price) is higher than the strike price.

Conversely, when you sell, short or "write" a call option, it gives the buyer, the right to buy that asset from you at the strike price anytime before the option expires. In this case the buyer will exercise his right / option only when the price in the market (spot price) is higher than the strike price and so you will be obliged to sell at loss.

We know that a premium needs to be paid by the option buyer to the option seller. It is called price of the option or the option premium.

Example:

We are in January and you buy 100 call options contract of XYZ stock with maturity on April 1. The price of the call option (or say option premium) is INR 1 a share. The listed spot price of XYZ stock is INR 50 and the strike price is INR 52 a share.

In effect you have got the right to buy 100 XYZ shares for INR 52 each by paying INR 100 (INR 1 x 100 shares). The seller on the other hand has received INR 100 and has agreed to sell 100 shares at of XYZ at INR 52 each if you choose to exercise your option.

Now if the price of XYZ share does not rise above INR 52 by April 1, the option is not exercised and you lose INR 100. But if the XYZ share price does well and you exercise the option when the stock price touches INR 60, you will be able to buy 100 shares at INR 52 when they are actually worth INR 60 each, making a gain. The price of the option will also rise reflecting this change in its underlying stock.

In case it is not an American option where you can exercise the option at any time before maturity, you are always free to sell the option itself in the market. Thus when the XYZ share price will reach INR 60 from INR 50, the price of call option will also increase. Say it reaches INR 5 from INR 1. You can now sell the option itself at INR 5 and lock gains instead of exercising the option first and then selling the shares.

PS: American Option allows exercise of option at any time before maturity whereas European Option allows exercise only at the time of option maturity.

Put Option:

A put option gives the holder the **right to sell** an asset by a certain date at a certain price. Put options are purchased by traders who think the price of the asset will go down. Similarly, put options are sold by traders who think the price of the asset will go up.

When you buy a put option, you are buying the right to sell an asset at a strike price also known as exercise price, regardless of what the price of that asset may be in future. As a put option buyer, you will exercise this option only when the strike price is higher than the price in the market (spot price).

Conversely, when you sell, short or "write" a put option, it gives the buyer, the right to sell that asset to you at the strike price anytime before the option expires. In this case the buyer will exercise his right / option only when the strike price is higher than the price in the market (spot price) and so you will be obliged to buy at loss.

Example:

We are in January and you buy 100 put options contract of XYZ stock with maturity on April 1. The price of the put option (or say option premium) is INR 1 a share. The listed spot price of XYZ stock is INR 50 and the strike price is INR 52 a share.

In effect you have got the right to sell 100 XYZ shares for INR 52 each by paying INR 100 (INR 1 x 100 shares). The seller on the other hand has received INR 100 and has agreed to buy 100 shares at of XYZ at INR 52 each if you choose to exercise your option.

Now if the price of XYZ share does not fall below INR 52 by April 1, the option is not exercised and you lose INR 100. But if the XYZ share price performs badly as anticipated by you and you exercise the option when stock price is at INR 45, you will be able to sell 100 shares at INR 52 when they are actually worth only INR 45 each, making a gain. The price of the option will also rise reflecting this change in its underlying stock and in case it is not an American option where you can exercise the option at any time before maturity, you are always free to sell the option itself in the market.

Please note that Options can be either In the Money (ITM) or Out of Money (OTM) which is only a matter of strike price's position vis-à-vis the current market price. An ITM option is one with a strike price that has already been surpassed by the current stock price, meaning the option has an intrinsic profit/value and its holder is more likely to turn a profit. An OTM option is one that has a strike price that the underlying security has yet to reach.

For example; In a call option, If the Current Price of XYZ share is INR 50 and the strike price is INR 100 (greater than INR 50), it is OTM whereas if the strike price is INR 40 (up to INR 50), it is ITM. Similarly, in a put option, If the Current Price of XYZ share is INR 50 and the strike price is INR 10, it is OTM whereas if the strike price is INR 60, it is ITM as you are already into profit.

Futures Contracts and Options as stated above are traded on a Stock Exchange and what's interesting about buying or selling in F&O segment is that you only pay for a percentage of the price of the contract that is called margin.

Let's now look at the use of F&O segment for Money Laundering and Tax Evasion purposes:

Modus Operandi 1: Low level of complexity

Participants in the scheme:

1. Mr Darkhorse who could be any of the following –
   a. A black money holder who simply wants to convert INR 1 Million of his black money into white and pay taxes on such earning.
   OR
   b. A black money holder who has got INR 1 Million of black money and has incurred an actual loss of INR 1 Mio which he wants to set-off from white money proceeds, thereby reducing tax impact on Money Laundering.
   OR
   c. A business man who wants to show some fictitious profits of say INR 1 Mio in his books of accounts to show it to his bankers, creditors, investors and other analysts.
2. Mr Whitehorse who could be any of the following –
   a. A businessman who has got some tax liability on his income/ profits/ Capital Gains and therefore wants to incur some fictitious losses of say INR 1 Mio so as avoid tax.
   OR
   b. A businessman who needs black money to pay for illicit expenditure like payment of bribes, kick backs etc.
3. M/s Jockey& Co. who is a stock broker with good knowledge of trading in derivatives and secretly earns a good amount of money from helping his clients in laundering money and evading taxes. In this illicit business, he is helped by many of his stock broker friends.

In a nutshell, Darkhorse as usual has black money which he wants to convert into white and Jockey and Whitehorse facilitate the transaction for their interests.

Darkhorse and Whitehorse approach Jockey for their purposes and the game begins:

Jockey chooses stock of XYZ Limited with following characteristics:

✓ The stock trades in Derivative segment. Thus an investor can trade in the F&O of XYZ Limited

✓ The stock is less volatile and is expected to remain stable during the course of the scheme.

✓ XYZ Limited is a small company which may or may not have considerable volumes in F&O segment but there are many expiry dates which are illiquid having very low trading volumes.

Suppose stock of XYZ Limited is trading at INR 200/- in cash segment (spot price) and the premium for its three months call option with strike price of INR 230/- is INR 20/-. The market lot size of XYZ options is 1000. It is thus an OTM option as the stock price is lower than strike price in a call option and it will be beneficial to exercise the option only when the stock price goes above INR 230/-. Being an OTM option in an ordinary company, away from limelight, that is exercisable after three months, it is almost illiquid with very few participants.

Jockey is the broker of both Darkhorse and Whitehorse who have authorised him to trade on their behalf.

1st leg of the transaction:

Jockey undertakes transactions in Call Options of XYZ Limited on behalf of Darkhorse and Whitehorse as follows:

Jockey buys 1000 Call Option contracts (call options) of XYZ Limited on behalf of Whitehorse and sells these contracts at the same time on behalf of Darkhorse as detailed in the table.

Call Options - XYZ Limited	
Spot Price	200
Strike Price	230
Option Price (1st Leg)	20
Lot Size	1,000
Lots bought & sold	1,000
Options bought & sold - 1 Mio (1000 x 1000)	1,000,000
Contract Amount - INR 20 Mio	20,000,000
Amount at which options bought by Whitehorse and sold by Darkhorse @INR 20 each - INR 20 Mio	20,000,000
Option Price traded for reversal (2nd Leg)	19
Reversal: Amount at which bought by Darkhorse and sold by Whitehorse - INR 19 each	19,000,000
Loss to Whitehorse and Gain to Darkhorse	1,000,000

Therefore Whitehorse pays premium of INR 20 Million (20*1000*1000) for underlying value of INR 200 Million (i.e. 200*1000*1000) which is received by Darkhorse.

It may be noted that Whitehorse need not have INR 20 Million in his account immediately for this pay-out as he only needs margin money @ 10% of the contract amount. Moreover, the contracts are settled in T+2 cycle and arranging finance for margin money is no problem for a broker especially for his favourite clients. Further, Jockey also knows that this trade will soon get settled through reversal.

What has essentially happened in the above transaction is that Whitehorse has bought an option/right to buy 1 Million (1,000,000) shares of XYZ Limited at INR 230 each which he will exercise if the share price of XYZ goes above INR 230 and Darkhorse would be obliged to sell these shares at INR 230 each if Whitehorse exercises his option.

2nd leg of the transaction:

After undertaking first leg of the transaction as stated above, Mr Jockey then squares off the position of both his clients before the stock fluctuates significantly. Whitehorse has bought the options so he has to sell the options to settle his long outstanding position and similarly Darkhorse has sold the options, so he has to buy the options to settle his short outstanding position.

Jockey will first watch the movement in the stock and the option price and decide upon the reversal accordingly, minimizing any room for suspicion.

For reversal of the trade, he bids to buy the outstanding 1000 Call option contracts on behalf of Darkhorse at INR 19/- each so as to square off his short position which he is carrying at INR 20/-. There won't be any interest in this bid as the price is lower than the market price (although not significantly) and the market is illiquid.

Simultaneously Jockey sells 1000 Call option contracts at INR 19/- on behalf of Mr Whitehorse which squares off his long position being carried at INR 20/-.

The transaction is summarised as follows:

XYZ Limited - Call Options							
	Date	Trade Time	Option Price	Cash/Spot Price	Contract Qty.	Seller	Buyer
1st Leg	Today	Just Now	20.00	200	10,00,000	Darkhorse	Whitehorse
2nd Leg	Today	30 Mins later	19.00	200	10,00,000	Whitehorse	Darkhorse

The outcome:

As a result of this transaction, Darkhorse has made a sweet profit of INR 1 Million [(INR 20 – INR 19) *1000 options*1000 lot size] and similarly Mr Whitehorse has incurred a loss of INR 1 Million. Trades Settled. Money Laundered.

What happens behind the scene is that Darkhorse hands over his black money of INR 1 Million to Jockey who then hands it over to Whitehorse. Darkhorse gets white money in lieu of his black money and Whitehorse incurs loss in his books of accounts. Purposes of both get solved.

Mr Jockey receives good amount of commission from both the parties.

Example II: The same transaction can also be done through Put Options:

Step 1: At 10:30 AM, Whitehorse, through Jockey buys 1000 lots of Put Options of ABC Ltd. at INR 20.50 which have been sold by Darkhorse.

Step 2: At 10:31 AM, before there could be any adverse change in the premium prices, Whitehorse reverses the trade and places Ask/Sell bid for 1000 lots of his put option which gets settled at INR 19.50 and the party is again Darkhorse and broker to both is Jockey.

	Date	Trade Time	Option Price	Cash/Spot Price	Contract Qty.	Seller	Buyer
ABC Limited - Put Options							
Step 1	23-Nov-16	10:30 AM	20.50	350	10,00,000	Darkhorse	Whitehorse
Step 2	23-Nov-16	10:31 AM	19.50	350	10,00,000	Whitehorse	Darkhorse

MODUS OPERANDI - 1

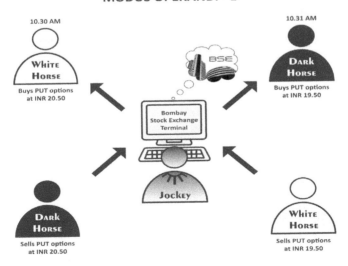

99

1000 lots of 1000 options is taken as hypothetical example for understanding purposes. In real scenarios, Jockey would have executed the above transaction in parts instead of one lump sum lot size. Moreover, in real scenarios, M/s Jockey & Co. is clever enough to place intermittent bids at INR 20.25 and INR 20 etc. before finally closing the 2nd leg of the transaction at INR 19.50 to form a trail and avoid suspicion.

As the trades above happen through Stock Exchange, the exchange itself becomes a facilitator of the Money Laundering exercise and since the prices at which transactions happened are not too distanced from the market prices, tax authorities and regulators find it complicated to connect these dots. Moreover, Darkhorse and Whitehorse may be sitting at different places and executing various such deals day in and day out in parts without the notice of tax authorities.

They even have their standard replies ready in case there is investigation. Whitehorse says that the trade in XYZ Limited was made erroneously and without full knowledge of the company and he rectified his mistake as soon as he became aware of it. On the other hand, Darkhorse has his own standard story to tell. He says that he never thought of squaring off his position until he got a very good opportunity. He just pounced over it and made a decent profit.

In such cases M/s Jockey & Co. needs to be caught who knows the full story and prepared the pitch for the game. His standard reply that he is just a broker who acted on the instructions of his clients won't be acceptable.

Modus Operandi 2: Higher level of complexity

In modus operandi 1, Jockey was a big bang broker who facilitated everything himself. However, in real life scenarios things are bound to be much more complicated with involvement of various brokers.

Let us take one more example where say 2 brokers join hands to do the same task as above (to keep it simple, else there can be many more brokers operating in unison).

Participants in the scheme:

Besides Darkhorse and Whitehorse who are present with their illicit motives mentioned earlier, there are two brokers – Jockey1 (J1) and Jockey2 (J2) who operate in a cartel.

For simplification, please note that Whitehorse who wants to incur artificial losses in his books of accounts is a client of J1 and Darkhorse who wants to launder his black money is a client of J2. In reality, it is difficult to find out who is a client of whom as both Darkhorse and Whitehorse have trading accounts with both J1 and J2.

1st leg of the transaction:

The first part of the modus operandi remains largely the same:

J1 and J2 zero in on stock of XYZ Limited. The stock trades at INR 200/- in cash segment (spot price) and option premium for its three months call option with strike price of INR 230/- is INR 20/-. The market lot size of XYZ options is 1000. Since it is an OTM option and exercisable after three months, it is almost illiquid with very few participants.

J1 undertakes transactions in Call Options of XYZ Limited. He bids for 1000 Call Option contracts (call options) of XYZ Limited at INR 20 each on behalf of Whitehorse. The transaction value comes to INR 20 Million (i.e. 20*1000*1000) for underlying value of INR 200 Million (i.e. 200*1000*1000).

Now the complexity in introduced in the game.

First disguise:

These 1000 call option contracts are sold by Darkhorse (to Whitehorse) but through J2 instead of J1.

2nd leg of the transaction:

After taking positions where Whitehorse is long 1000 contracts and Darkhorse is short 1000 contracts, it's time to square off of the positions as mentioned in the previous modus operandi.

Second disguise:

Here J1 reverses the position of Darkhorse and J2 reverses the position of Whitehorse. Got it?

> It means that before reversing the positions in this trade, J1 and J2 have reversed their clients.

To simplify, Whitehorse who was the client of J1 in the first leg of transaction has become client of J2 while reversing his position. Similarly Darkhorse has squared off his position through J1 whereas he took his initial position through J2.

The game is essentially being played by J1 and J2 where Darkhorse and Whitehorse are meek spectators who are happy signing off the contract notes sent to them.

Mr Jockey1 reverses the trade as under:

On behalf of Darkhorse, he bids to buy the 1000 Call option contracts at INR 19/- so as to square off his short position of 1000 call options that he was carrying at INR 20/-.

J2 who is watching the above transaction on his screen immediately sells 1000 Call option contracts at INR 19/- on behalf of Whitehorse and accordingly squares off his long position of 1000 call options that he was carrying at INR 20/-.

A pictorial depiction of the same is as under:

Step 1: At 10:30 AM, Whitehorse, through J1 buys 1000 lots of Call Options of XYZ Ltd. at INR 20 each which have been sold by Darkhorse through J2.

Step 2: At 10:31 AM, before there could be any adverse change in the premium prices, Whitehorse reverses the trade and places Ask/Sell bid for his 1000 lots through J2 which gets settled at INR 19 and the party is again Darkhorse but the broker to Darkhorse is J1.

MODUS OPERANDI - 2

Outcome: The same but with a tinge of added complexity.

The result of this transaction is same, Mr Darkhorse has made a sweet fake profit of INR 1 Million [(INR 20 – INR 19) *1000 options*1000 lot size] in his books of accounts and similarly Mr Whitehorse has incurred a loss of INR 1 Million. Trades Settled. Money Laundered.

What happened behind the scene is also same - Darkhorse hands over his black money of INR 1 Million to J1 who forwards it to Whitehorse. Purposes of both get solved. Game Over.

It may be noted that the trades are reversed at the same time or different times depending upon the liquidity and price levels of the options.

J1 and J2 share the commission received from both the parties as per their mutual terms.

POINTS TO PONDER:

$ In reality, these schemes will be more fiendish and complex than that stated here.

$ Those of you who might be thinking about the possible (mis)use of 'Futures' too in the same manner as 'options' mentioned above, please note that futures prices is linked to cash segment price in a linear manner as opposed to 'Options' price which involves various other factors like Time To expiry, Volatility, Strike Price etc. It is the play of these many factors in options price which helps obfuscate the manipulation and leads to its abuse. The abuse of Futures is presented in the next part of this chapter.

$ In India, SEBI (Securities and Exchange Board of India) is well aware of these schemes and investigates the transactions where brokers buy/sell almost equal quantities of contracts in a synchronised manner. Thus, brokers indulging in non-genuine trades will be prosecuted under various laws and also lose their license.

METHOD 16-B

Derivative Trading — Futures & Options (F&O) Segment

Part-2

In the previous chapter we discussed the abuse of Options (in the F&O segment) for Money Laundering. In this chapter we will discuss another abuse of the F&O segment where 'Futures' serve as Alternate Borrowing and Lending mechanism.

Here the lending and borrowing transaction remains undisclosed. Its true form is neither reflected in the lender's financial statements nor in the borrower's financial statements.

The modus operandi: Futures Market (F&O) segment for Off-Balance Sheet Borrowing

Participants in the scheme:

1. Mr Raghu who is in need of funds of INR 1 Million but he does not want to show this as debt in his Balance Sheet.

2. M/s John & Co. who is a stock broker and has surplus funds. He uses his surplus funds for lending to people and earns interest and commission via such lending but that remains under wraps in his books of accounts. In this illicit business, he is helped by many of his stock broker friends.

Raghu approaches John and John agrees to lend INR 1 Mio to Raghu with interest @ 12% p.a. However, the lending in this case is not simply transfer of money from lender to borrower. It happens through trading of a Small to Medium sized company's stock (say Wellness Limited) over the Stock Exchange.

(Please note that stock of Wellness Limited has been selected after careful research. The company is listed on F&O segment of the Stock Exchange. Its futures are traded but with low level of liquidity i.e. the trading volumes remain low and the company is away from limelight).

The game begins:

John asks Raghu to short sell 50,000 shares of Wellness Limited at its prevailing market price of INR 20/- per share in the futures market for a period of 6 months.

Raghu, as directed, places a short sell bid to short sell 50,000 shares of Wellness Limited at INR 20 each. John with or without his cartel of stock brokers places the off-setting buy bid and buys the stock from Raghu in the futures market at INR 20.

Raghu thus receives INR 1 Million (INR 20 x 50,000 shares) and John has got the stock (50,000 shares) in futures market.

Short selling as mentioned here simply means selling an asset that is not owned. It is possible for some –but not all – investment assets.

Now the deal between John and Raghu is that after an agreed upon period (which can range anywhere from 1 month to 12 months), Raghu will return the money with interest @12% p.a.

So say after 6 months, Raghu wants to return the money – INR 1 Mio along with interest accrued of INR 60,000/- (12% * INR 1 Million * 0.5 years) to John.

He therefore buys back 50,000 shares from John and his cartel at INR 21.20/- per share. For this purpose, John and his cartel place sell bid in the futures market at this price and Raghu obeys the order by placing an off-setting buy bid at INR 21.20/-. Positions settled. Repayment Done. Transaction complete.

The outcome:

In the books of accounts, the transaction would appear as sale and purchase of stock (investment transaction) whereas it was actually a lending and borrowing transaction between the parties.

Books will show the interest amount of INR 60,000/- as STCG in case of John and Short Term Capital Loss of INR 60,000/- in case of Raghu. His Leverage in Books or Debt to Equity Ratio remains unaffected and he can use the loss to set-off any other eligible Capital Gain, if any.

It goes without saying that in real scenarios, such a deal will be more complicated.

METHOD 17

Change of Client Code in Trading in Real Contract Note

Sometimes the rules are not made too stringent, considering that there should be minimal inconvenience to those who follow them diligently but then some unscrupulous people are always out there to take advantage of the loopholes present in the rules.

The aforementioned method exploits the window provided by the bourses including stock exchanges, commodity and FOREX exchanges for rectification of any genuine errors made by the brokers.

Here a broker connives with the parties at both ends (buying and selling) of the transaction that is undertaken by him to provide undue benefit to both of them.

Let me explain this method by way of an example:

The modus operandi:

Darkhorse has good amount of black money and he now wants to buy a big condominium in a posh high rise building. The seller of the house demands white money which is not there with Darkhorse. He would have definitely dumped this house for another one but for the love shown by his wife for this house, he is willing to search some avenues where he can launder his black money into white. He also needs to launder money extremely fast else he faces serious trouble from his wife.

Suppose he is short of just INR 1 Million in white money and approaches Jockey who has the reputation of being a shrewd and corrupt stock broker. Jockey agrees to help Darkhorse in his misdemeanour and opens his dematerialised share trading account.

Jockey knows many of his clients who keep on making big money by trading stocks in cash as well as F&O segment. In F&O segment, especially in futures, the gains (and even losses) are higher than those in cash segment.

Jockey finds out that Whitehorse, who is one of his clients has made a huge profit of INR 1 Million today by short selling some shares (share lots) in a falling market. His profit is taxable @30% (say) as per the extant Income Tax Rules reducing his gain to INR 0.70 Million only.

Jockey persuades Whitehorse to sell his profit to him and he will share his tax liability over it.

Jockey pays him INR 0.80 Million in black money which he receives from Darkhorse. Whitehorse moves out of the game, silently but happily.

At the end of the day/ trading hours, while final reporting of the transaction to the Stock Exchange, Jockey swaps the client codes in this transaction. He replaces the client code of Whitehorse with that of Darkhorse, registering this transaction in his name and shows that the name of Whitehorse was punched in erroneously which is now being rectified. This happens within minutes from the end of the trading hours.

Here, either client code for both legs of the transaction is modified/ rectified if Money Laundering deal is struck after full transaction or for only 1st leg of the transaction i.e. short selling, if the deal is struck before squaring off the transaction by monitoring its ITM position.

Thus all the gains from this transaction get transferred to Darkhorse with no objection from Whitehorse who remains silent after getting his due share. Money Laundered.

Darkhorse gets INR 1 Mio of Capital Gains through a real contract note. He gave INR 1 Mio in black money to Jockey who gave INR 0.80 Mio to Whitehorse and kept INR 0.20 Mio as his commission.

The sharing in the deal is structured by the parties as per mutually beneficial terms. It may further be noted that instead of laundering the entire black money of INR 1 Mio at once, Jockey would split it into many trades of smaller amounts and spread over many days so as to avoid regulatory attention.

POINTS TO PONDER:

- $ Securities and Exchange Board of India (SEBI) allowed a window of 30 minutes after the market closes to rectify any punching errors by brokers. This window was misused by some brokers in the manner stated above. The regulator has since issued strictures on the practice which has now made this method difficult.

- $ Stock Exchanges now impose hefty penalties on modification of client codes.

- $ Further, Stock Exchanges do not delete the trail of the transaction. The original client code therefore can be made available to tax investigators as and when required.

- $ A genuine purpose is mandatory for carrying out client code modification.

- $ Income Tax Department knows of this method and has issued notices to hundreds of brokers for altering the client codes in this practice which is illegal. It requires all the stock exchanges to provide a monthly report of all client code modifications.

METHOD 18

Small Merger & Acquisition (M&A)

A M&A transaction refers to one company acquiring another company or two or more companies getting merged together to form a third company. M & A transactions are strictly governed in all countries and various approvals are required to take it through.

However, a M&A deal in Money Laundering industry is devoid of many difficulties that arise in a regular one because everything is fabricated to look like real. The target and acquiring companies are hand in glove, the purchase consideration is already known and above all the purpose is not to identify synergies but to launder black into white.

Why this method is called a 'small' M&A transaction is because:

✓ The chances of scrutiny by tax authorities,

✓ The level of detail in which all stakeholders delve in and

✓ The degree of transparency expected

in a 'small' M&A transaction are all pretty much lower than that involved in a large M&A transaction and therefore it suits the interests of a money launderer.

Let us check the ways in which Money Laundering is done through M&A

Modus Operandi 1: The crude way

Mr Darkhorse has INR 1 Million of black money which he wants to convert into white.

He approaches Mr Jockey and as usual they decide to take the government rules for a ride.

Jockey floats a small unlisted company for the purpose in the name of ATPL (All Trades Private Limited) in which Darkhorse is a shareholder along with his wife (for the sake of minimum requirement of two shareholders). ATPL has issued say 25,000 shares each to Darkhorse and his wife at the Face Value of INR 10/- per share.

This money of INR 500,000/- (25,000 shares x INR 10 x 2 shareholders) will either remain in the company's account or transferred to some other firms managed by Jockey and his group as loan or investment.

The Balance Sheet of ATPL thus looks similar to this:

ATPL

Liabilities	Amount (INR)	Assets	Amount (INR)
Equity Share Capital 50,000 shares of Face Value INR 10 each	5,00,000	Cash/ Loans and Advances/ Investments	5,00,000
Total	5,00,000	Total	5,00,000

ATPL can be a firm or an existing company also for the purpose of this transaction.

Besides helping float or find ATPL for Mr Darkhorse, there are other services also that are provided by Jockey. First he does some genuinely appearing business transactions in ATPL so as to enhance its artificial valuation. Then he tells Darkhorse about a listed company – XYZ Limited which will help him launder his money.

XYZ Limited is a big company and requires some black money to get new orders from government.

XYZ Limited agrees to buy ATPL. The purchase consideration is decided at INR 1,500,000/- i.e. INR 30 per share which translates to a premium of 2 times over the actual share price of INR 10 each. Needless to say that XYZ Limited does so only after receiving INR 1,000,000/- of black money from Darkhorse. INR 500,000 worth of assets is already stored in ATPL.

Darkhorse and his wife get INR 1,500,000 (One and a Half Million) through cheque/wire transfer i.e. White Money. Money Laundered.

We know that parties are free to decide the sale-purchase terms on their own and if required, a valuation certificate from a Chartered Accountant/ Valuer friend can anytime be arranged valuing this company at a steep premium due to a brilliant business idea or business model it possesses leading to robust future cash flows.

It may be noted that Mr Jockey and his team are specialist in amalgamations of companies for Money Laundering purposes. They do everything it takes to get ATPL merged into XYZ including the High Court approval. After all, the court too is bound by the rules. So if there is a No Objection Certificate from the creditors and other stakeholders, the management may go ahead with a merger, demerger or any other restructuring exercise.

Moreover, the object clause of ATPL can be changed any time to sync in line with that of XYZ Limited. This makes it easier to explain and justify the merger/ amalgamation transaction in front of any one.

Modus Operandi 2: The sophisticated way

In the above example, the money paid by XYZ Limited as purchase consideration – INR 1.50 Mio through bank account may leave ample room for getting caught in an investigation. Therefore launderers have devised a more sophisticated way of executing this transaction.

Here Jockey asks the promoters/ management of XYZ Limited to buy out ATPL at its actual value only i.e. at its Face Value of INR 1 Million in an all-stock deal.

XYZ Limited in this case is a small listed company, whose promoters are completely hand in glove with M/s Jockey & Co. in their illegitimate business of laundering money.

All-stock deal means that XYZ Limited will pay whole of the purchase consideration by issuing its own shares instead of cash/ bank transfer.

If the share price of XYZ Limited is trading at INR 50/- at the time of this takeover and the fair value of 1 share of ATPL is equal to its Face Value of INR 10/-; the swap ratio comes to 5:1. It means every shareholder in ATPL gets 1 share in XYZ Limited for every 5 shares they hold in ATPL.

Accordingly, Darkhorse and his wife receive 5,000 shares each (25000 ÷ 5) of XYZ in lieu of their shareholding in ATPL.

After obtaining the M&A approvals and allotment of shares, the black money is transferred from Darkhorse to M/s Jockey & Co. which is then smurfed into various bank accounts of Jockey and his affiliates. Jockey & Co. uses this money to artificially inflate the price of XYZ to some predetermined level through the Circular Trading method as discussed in the chapter on Penny Stocks.

The price of XYZ reaches INR 150/- in a few months or a year due to combined efforts of Jockey's cartel and XYZ's management.

Now Jockey calls upon Darkhorse to sell his 10,000 shares (his wife's shares combined) in XYZ Ltd. Darkhorse sells these shares at INR 150/- each to Jockey and his group.

The result - Darkhorse is able to show a Capital Gain Profit of INR 1,000,000 (150 x 10,000 shares – 500,000 of original investment). Money Laundered.

METHOD 19

Share Premium Companies

Share Premium also known as securities premium is the excess amount that the investor (shareholder) pays to the company to acquire its shares over and above the Face Value of its shares.

Example: If the Face Value of one share of a company is INR 10 and an investor buys shares of the company at INR 15 each, then INR 5 is the securities premium per share that gets credited to Securities Premium Account. This surplus amount cannot be used by the company for distribution of dividends to shareholders and has other restrictions too over its application. It can however be used for purposes like Issuance of Bonus Shares; Buy-Back of shares, Writing Off of certain Preliminary expenses etc.

Let us see the role share premium plays in the Money Laundering industry.

The modus operandi:

Darkhorse wants to convert INR 1 Mio of his black money into white. He with the help of Jockey has incorporated a company – Farce Private Ltd. for the purpose.

The Balance Sheet of Farce Private Limited on a given date is as follows:

Farce Private Limited

Liabilities	Amount(INR)	Assets	Amount(INR)
Equity		Assets	
Share Capital 200,000 shares of INR 10 each	2,000,000	Fixed Assets, Bank Accounts, Investments etc.	2,200,000
Surplus Reserves Profit and Loss Account	200,000		
Total	**2,200,000**	**Total**	**2,200,000**

Darkhorse and his family members /trusted aides own 100% share capital in Farce Limited. Farce Limited is generally a Shell Company with no or negligible business and works as a front company for Money Laundering purposes. Accordingly it has a small profit in its reserves.

Now Mr Whitehorse pitches in. Darkhorse hands over his INR 1 Mio of black money to him and Whitehorse in return agrees to buy fresh 5% stake in Farce Limited which is a profitable company (see it has surplus profit in its Balance Sheet) at INR 100 per share through preferential allotment. It means that he is willing to pay a share premium of INR 90 per share. *A valuation certificate, if required is arranged from a Chartered Accountant friend basis discounted value of huge cash flows in future.*

Accordingly, Whitehorse after finding Farce a very promising company for future buys 10,000 shares (5% stake prior to issuance of fresh shares) at INR 1 Million (10,000 shares x INR 100 each). He transfers this amount to the account of Farce Private Limited through cheque or wire transfer.

Farce issues fresh share capital of INR 100,000 (10,000 shares x INR 10 each) and records INR 900,000 (10,000 shares x INR 90 each) as securities premium in its books of accounts.

Now the Balance Sheet of Farce Private Limited will look as follows:

Farce Private Limited

Liabilities	Amount(INR)	Assets	Amount(INR)
Equity		Assets	
Share Capital 210,000 shares of INR 10 each	2,100,000	Fixed Assets, Bank Accounts, Investments etc. (Existing) + INR 1 Mio (Addition)	3,200,000
Share Premium Account	900,000		
Surplus Reserves Profit and Loss Account	200,000		
Total	3,200,000	Total	3,200,000

In this way, Darkhorse receives INR 1 Mio of white money in the company which he fully controls. *Had Whitehorse acquired 5% stake in Farce Limited through purchase of shares from Darkhorse, it would have resulted into tax on the Capital Gain made by Darkhorse.*

The shareholding pattern of Farce Private Limited now stands as under:

Shareholders	Shares subscribed	Shareholding (%)
Darkhorse and his family	200,000 shares of Face Value INR 10 each	95.2%
Whitehorse	10,000 shares of Face Value INR 10 each	4.8%
Total	**210,000 shares of Face Value INR 10 each**	**100%**

The story does not end here. Going forward, Darkhorse wants to retain full control of the company without parting with the aforementioned 4.8%. For this purpose, he needs to buy back the shareholding of Whitehorse. He decides to buy all the shares back at their Fair Market Value (FMV).

In this case (considering that Balance Sheet reflects the Fair Values), the FMV per share of Farce Limited comes to INR 15.24 (Net Asset Value (NAV) of INR 3.20 Million ÷ 2,10,000 shares). Thus Whitehorse sells his 10,000 shares at INR 1,52,400 to Darkhorse and family.

Darkhorse transfers this amount in white money to Whitehorse as purchase consideration who then hands over the equivalent black money to Darkhorse. In effect, Darkhorse has laundered black money of INR 8,47,600 (INR 1,000,000 – 1,52,400) into white money.

In real scenarios, instead of one single Whitehorse there would be 40 to 50 persons who will pool in their white money to launder big sums of black money and Darkhorse will buy back his shares only after a reasonable period has elapsed from issuance of shares.

POINTS TO PONDER:

$ Revisions to Income Tax Act 1961 have curbed the aforesaid practice by stating that any amount received by a company in the above manner whether through share premium, share application or by any other name shall be deemed to be the income of the company and hence taxable. However, this provision exempts shares issued at premium to non-residents and venture capital funds and thus still attracts money launderers a bit.

$ The premise for exempting Non-Residents is that the flow of their money in foreign currency would be monitored by Reserve Bank of India but this has still left a loop hole open for money launderers who have connections with non-resident persons (including off-shore companies) or venture capital companies for whom they channelize funds abroad through Hawala and other alternative remittance modes.

$ Subscription of shares in the manner stated above falls under Private Placement route available to companies to raise funds which has undergone stringent revisions under Companies Act 2013 making its abuse difficult. Use of Private Placement of shares as a means in money laundering is further discussed in detail in a separate chapter.

$ In wake of the above, the abuse of this method has been stopped to the maximum extent.

METHOD 20

Convertible Financial Instruments

As mentioned in the Points To Ponder section of the previous chapter that revisions to Income Tax Act 1961 have curbed the use of Share Premium method in tax free laundering of money in the manner stated therein.

The said revision to Income Tax Act says that if any sum is found credited in the books of a closely held company i.e. a private limited company in the name of share application money, share premium, share capital or by any other name, then no explanation offered by the company shall be deemed to be satisfactory by the tax officer and hence this sum will be taxable as income of the company unless:

(a) The credit has come from a Non-Resident of India who offers an explanation for the same or

(b) The credit has come from a venture capital fund or venture capital company or

(c) The tax officer is convinced about the genuineness of the sources of such credit.

Therefore the first loophole is that if a Non-Resident of India (say a Foreign Company or a person who has lived in India for less than 180 days in a year) or a Venture Capitalist is hand in glove with the money launderer, then the Share Premium method is open for misuse.

The other loophole is issuance of convertible securities like a Convertible Bond.

Since Convertible Bond is a debt instrument and not share capital in nature, the use of its potential in bypassing the aforementioned regulation cannot be ruled out.

A Convertible Bond is a debt which can be converted into a predetermined amount of company's shares subject to fulfilment of certain conditions. It means that the bondholder has got the right to convert his bond into equity shares of the company if some previously agreed upon criterion is fulfilled.

For example: XYZ Limited has issued Convertible Bond of INR 1000 Face Value that is convertible into its equity shares after a period of 3 years provided the company is profit making. The bond has a coupon of 8% p.a. payable annually. Bond's agreement also specifies a conversion ratio which is the number of shares that the investor will receive if he chooses to convert. If the bond has a conversion ratio of 20, the investor will get 20 shares per bond in XYZ after 3 years and thus his effective cost would be INR 50 per share (INR1000 / 20 = INR 50).

As this bond is issued by a closely held company, it casts a shadow of doubt over the transparency of the agreement between the company and the investor (bond holder).

The modus operandi:

Darkhorse wants to convert INR 1 Mio of his black money into white. He with the help of Jockey has incorporated a company – Farce Private Ltd. for the purpose.

The Balance Sheet of Farce Private Limited on a given date is as follows:

Farce Private Limited

Liabilities	Amount(INR)	Assets	Amount(INR)
Equity		Assets	
Share Capital 200,000 shares of INR 10 each	2,000,000	Fixed Assets, Bank Accounts, Investments etc.	2,000,000
Total	**2,000,000**	**Total**	**2,000,000**

Darkhorse and his family members /trusted aides own 100% share capital in Farce Limited. Farce Limited is generally a Shell Company with no or negligible business and works as a front company for Money Laundering purposes.

Now Mr Whitehorse pitches in. Darkhorse hands over his INR 1 Mio of black money to Whitehorse who in turn invests INR 1 Mio in Farce Private Limited in white money. Darkhorse receives INR 1 Mio of White Money in the company that is 100% under his control. Money Laundered tax free since the amount received via Convertible Bond/ debt is not taxable in the hands of the company.

Here Whitehorse invests the amount through convertible bonds bearing coupon rate of 8% p.a. The amount invested will be a debt for 3 years after which it shall be converted into equity provided Farce Limited is into profits.

Every year, White horse will earn INR 80,000/- (8% x INR 1 Million) as interest on his investment and an equal amount will be sent by him to Darkhorse in black money. Needless to mention that Whitehorse and Jockey receive good commission for facilitating this Money Laundering. All the documents including bond agreement are prepared in an organised way and TDS is deducted on the interest amount paid to Whitehorse to make the transaction appear completely genuine.

Rest of the story remains the same as stated in Share Premium method.

POINTS TO PONDER:

$ Since the income tax provision exempts non-residents and venture capitalists, convertibles are issued to these two categories for money laundering and Black Money of Darkhorse, if stashed overseas also finds a way to come to India in this manner through non-residents.

$ Tax Officials have full power to question this modus operandi and if un-satisfied with the genuineness of the transaction, treat the amount invested in form of convertibles as taxable income of the company.

$ As per the new Companies Act 2013, issuance of convertibles will fall under preferential allotment of securities and thus all its provisions shall apply. Preferential Allotment of securities is dealt with hereafter under Method 23.

METHOD 21

Stake Sale at Discount

I t is not just the share premium that facilitated laundering of black money as seen in the previous chapter, buying shares at discount too enabled money laundering as stated below:

The modus operandi:

Please have a look at the following Balance Sheet:

Farce Private Limited

Liabilities	Amount (INR)	Assets	Amount (INR)
Equity		Fixed Assets	
Share Capital 250,000 of INR 10 each	2,500,000	Furniture and Fixtures	500,000
Accumulated Losses	(1,000,000)	Cash-in-hand, Bank Balance and Investments in other companies	1,000,000
Current Liabilities	500,000	Current Assets	500,000
Total	**2,000,000**	**Total**	**2,000,000**

It is true that in real life scenarios, it will not be as simple a Balance Sheet as shown above and there will be plenty more items appearing than just those above so as to confuse the analysts and disguise the real purpose of its incorporation but the basic tents anyways would be the same as discussed here.

Farce Private Limited is 100% owned by Jockey and family. Farce is generally a Shell Company with no or negligible business and works as a front end company for Money Laundering purposes. The company shows accumulated loss because it is to be sold in future at a steep discount which gets justified on account of its loss making business. *(Please note that it won't be the company as such that will be sold but the shareholding therein.)*

It may be noted that the accumulated losses shown above are actually fictitious losses only *(Please refer to chapter on onshore Shell Corporations for detailed understanding)*. These may be in form of purchases, expenditures or bad debts written off etc. that will get recovered at a later date and reversed to revenue/profit and loss account once the control of the company passes on to Darkhorse.

In real scenarios, many such companies are held by various Jockeys who wait for some Darkhorse to approach them for laundering their illicit black money.

When Mr Darkhorse approaches him with black money of INR 1 Million to get laundered, Jockey agrees to sell his shares in Farce Private Limited.

Jockey agrees to sell all the shares of Farce Private Limited to Darkhorse at INR 2/- per share i.e. at a discount of INR 8 each from Face Value and at a discount of INR 4/- per share from *on paper* Net Assets Value of INR 6/- per share [(INR 2.5 Mio – Loss of INR 1 Mio) ÷ 250,000 shares]. Parties are free to decide the sale-purchase terms on their own and if required, a valuation certificate from a Chartered Accountant friend is also arranged valuing this company at steep discount due to its loss making future cash flows (discounted cash flow method).

The full transaction is therefore that Jockey has sold his entire shareholding in Farce to Darkhorse for INR 500,000 (INR 2/- per share x 250,000 shares) in white money through cheque/wire transfer and balance INR 1,000,000/- in black money. Note from Balance Sheet above that INR 1,500,000 is the true value of the company. Moreover, the losses in the Balance Sheet are also fictitious and will get reversed/recovered at a later date.

The effect of this transaction is that Darkhorse gets 100% control over a company that has around INR 1.50 to INR 2 Million in well accounted for white money which can be in form of cash-in-hand, cash at bank or investments in other assets or companies as well as fictitious expenditures and losses. Jockey may get some capital loss along with tax benefit on the same depending upon the price at which he bought the shares in Farce Private Limited. Money Laundered.

In case, there are investments made by Farce Private Limited, Jockey completely assists in realizing the value of such investments and getting the amount credited to the bank accounts of the company as and when required by Darkhorse.

✓ It is interesting to see how the white money is routed in this company which is discussed in the chapter on Onshore Shell Companies.

✓ Once a company like Farce Private Limited was sold to Darkhorse, it was difficult for Income Tax Authorities to investigate & enquire about the source of funds in this company from Darkhorse. Jockey might have even relocated to avoid being summoned & questioned but things have changed with the advent of Union Budget 2017.

✓ Now Union Budget 2017 has brought out changes to plug these gaps. Previously, companies like Farce Private Limited were used as a commodity by entry operators like Jockey. A person would buy these companies as he would buy any other commodity with Black & White Money. However now sale of share at less than its Fair Market Value will attract tax and a professional giving wrong valuation certificate will be penalised strictly.

POINTS TO PONDER:

$ As stated in Method-12: Shell Corporations; the Union Budget of 2017 has given a huge blow to this method by stating that if the sale amount for transfer of unquoted share of a company is less than the Fair Market Value (FMV) of such share, the FMV of such share will be taken as sale amount and taxed accordingly. Moreover, if any professional – Chartered Accountant, Merchant Banker or Valuer gives incorrect information in his report or certificate then such professional will be liable for penalty.

$ Thus, if The Income Tax Department could find out that the purchases and other expenditures and losses of Farce Private Limited are fictitious, then they may charge tax on Jockey (the seller of Farce Pvt. Ltd.)

$ Moreover, if there is any accumulated loss in Farce Pvt. Ltd then such loss will also not be allowed to be carried forward and give further tax benefit in future years when the shareholding of the company is transferred from Whitehorse to Darkhorse unless and until Farce Pvt. Ltd. is a small company with turnover not exceeding INR 250 Million and eligible as a start-up i.e. incorporated between 01-Apr-2016 and 31-Mar-2019. This gives a boost to start ups but leaves a loophole which government needs to plug in.

METHOD 22

Evasion of Stamp Duty Tax

In the previous chapter, we discussed about Money Laundering through transfer of shares at discount. It may be noted that it is not just Money Laundering which is facilitated through transfer of shares but transfer of shares can lead to evasion of tax too.

Many such schemes are carefully crafted to evade taxes. In this case, it is stamp duty payable on transfer of property. Let us see how.

The modus operandi:

Please have a look at the following Balance Sheet:

Farce Private Limited

Liabilities	Amount (INR)	Assets	Amount (INR)
Equity		Fixed Assets	
Share Capital 1,500,000 of INR 10 each	15,000,000	Furniture and Fixtures	500,000
Current Liabilities	1,000,000	Property – Plot of land (Acquisition Price)	15,000,000
		Current Assets	500,000
Total	**16,000,000**	**Total**	**16,000,000**

Farce Private Limited is 100% owned by Darkhorse and family. Farce is generally a Shell Company with no business. The company has been incorporated only for the purpose of evading stamp duty on sale of its only asset – Land. Instead of holding Land in this personal name, Darkhorse holds it through his company.

Now Darkhorse wants to sell this land and finds a buyer in Whitehorse who is not interested in the business of Farce Private Limited but in the land held by it. He asks Whitehorse to buy entire shareholding in Farce Private Limited which owns that particular piece of land.

The effect is that the immovable property remains the property of Farce Private Limited with its title vesting in Farce Private Limited only but Whitehorse replaces Darkhorse as the shareholder as well as Director in Farce Private Limited. So in effect both the company owning the land and the land itself, comes under the control of Darkhorse.

In this transaction, there is stamp duty implication on transfer of shares from Darkhorse to Whitehorse but the rate of stamp duty on share transfer is generally miniscule compared to that on registration of conveyance deed in favour of Whitehorse.

The result however remains the same. If Whitehorse buys plot of directly from any seller, he becomes the owner of the property by virtue of conveyance deed registered in his favour. If he buys the same land through transfer of shares in the company that owns it, he becomes the owner of the land by virtue of 100% owner of that company that owns the land and the title thereto.

Since stamp duty is generally paid by the buyer, the stamp duty amount gets saved by buyer and therefore the asset held through a company becomes more attractive to him and a win-win proposition for both buyer and seller at the cost of the exchequer.

In India, Stamp Duty on transfer of shares is normally payable @0.25% whereas stamp duty payable on registration of sale deed/ conveyance deed executed between Darkhorse and Whitehorse can attract stamp duty anywhere from 6% to 14%.

Thus the transaction stated above enables a saving of anywhere from INR 8,62,500 [(6%-0.25%)*15,000,0000] to INR 20,62,500 [(14%-0.25%)*10,000,0000] which is shared between Darkhorse and Whitehorse in a mutually agreed ratio. To accentuate this, please note that stamp duty at say 0.25% on share transfer is payable on the value of share which is calculated based upon its book value and companies like Farce Private Limited will generally not state the value of its property at Market Value in its books of accounts, thereby enhancing the gains to the parties even further.

This method is abused not just in India but even in advanced countries wherever a similar anomaly exists between the stamp duty rates on registration of conveyance deed of property and registration of transfer of shares.

New set of rules are required to plug this gap completely.

METHOD 23

Private Placement or Preferential Allotment of Securities

It's said that the wrong doers do it privately and secretly. May be true; but private placement of shares has never been a secretive method used by money launderers in converting black money into white.

Private Placement or Preferential Allotment of shares *(taking them as same for this chapter)* means any offer or invitation given to select group of investors by a company to subscribe to its securities.

Here money is raised only from a select group of investors whereas in public issue, the offer to subscribe to the company's securities is made to the public at large and anyone who feels interested can apply. It is however not always feasible for a small company to issue securities to the general public since it is a time consuming and expensive option which attracts the attention of everyone and therefore is not much suitable for Money Laundering purposes.

Private placement of shares is made through a private placement offer letter addressed to a particular person or group from whom the company wants to raise funds and only they who are addressed to, can accept it. It means no one except the intended person can subscribe to the offer.

Investors here can be friends, relatives, directors, promoters, existing institutional investors including banks, Private Equity or Venture Capital funds etc. For the purpose of Money Laundering however, it will be the investor who has black money and wants to launder the same into white.

Private Placement of securities can be done by both listed as well as private companies. Undoubtedly the regulations are more stringent for listed companies than unlisted companies but both listed as well as unlisted company structures are open to abuse through this method. The company used however would be of small size in both the scenarios.

The modus operandi:

Participants in the scheme:

Mr Darkhorse – a black money holder. He has INR 1 Mio of black money which he wants to convert into white.

M/s Jockey and Co. – a black money operator or *Angadia*. His cartel owns and controls various shell companies, one of which is Farce Limited. In his Money Laundering adventures, Jockey is assisted by various stock market brokers.

Darkhorse shakes hands with Jockey and the game begins.

The Balance Sheet of Farce Limited on a given date is as follows:

Farce Limited

Liabilities	Amount (INR)	Assets	Amount (INR)
Equity			
Share Capital	5,000,000	Fixed Assets	1,500,000
500,000 of INR 10 each			
Reserves and Surplus		Cash-in-Hand, Bank Account and Investments	4,500,000
Profit and Loss Account	1,000,000		
Current Liabilities	500,000	Other Current Assets	500,000
Total	**6,500,000**	**Total**	**6,500,000**

Farce Limited can be a closely held company 100% owned by M/s Jockey & Co. or by his trusted lieutenants.

Alternatively, Farce can also be a publicly listed company that is small in size and whose promoters are gullible enough to connive in Money Laundering for a commission.

This company is used as a vehicle to deposit illegitimate cash into the bank accounts under the garb of its business proceeds.

Now Farce issues 10,000 shares to Darkhorse as preferential allotment at its Face Value of INR 10/- each. *If required, a valuation certificate valuing the price of the shares being issued (at par in this case) is easily arranged from a CA friend.*

MODUS OPERANDI

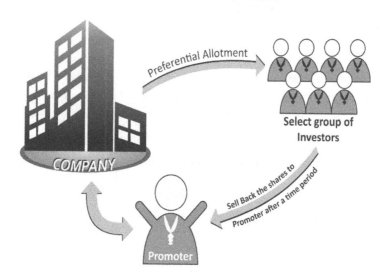

Darkhorse thus invests INR 1,00,000/- [10,000 shares x INR 10 each] as share capital into the company from his white money or through a loan arranged by Mr Jockey if he is white money starved. He therefore gets a small 1.96% stake in the company (10,000 shares ÷ 510,000 shares).

The Balance Sheet of Farce Limited now appears as under:

Farce Limited

Liabilities	Amount (INR)	Assets	Amount (INR)
Equity			
Share Capital 510,000 of INR 10 each	5,100,000	Fixed Assets	1,500,000
Reserves and Surplus		Cash-in-Hand, Bank Account and Investments	4,600,000
Profit and Loss Account	1,000,000		
Current Liabilities	500,000	Other Current Assets	500,000
Total	**6,600,000**	**Total**	**6,600,000**

As Farce can be both – a listed company as well as an unlisted company, let us discuss the modi operandi in both the scenarios.

Next step is actually a phase which takes some good amount of time required to give an authentic look to the whole scheme.

Scenario 1: Farce is a unlisted / closely held company:

If Farce Limited is a closely held company, its revenues and profitability will now see manifold increase, thanks to the business skills of M/s Jockey & Co. who will show artificial increase in revenues of Farce through deposit of illegal cash in bank accounts. The restaurant or the other bogus business it operates will show solid profits with regular cash deposits in company's bank accounts. The deposits are carefully broken down to less than INR 50,000/- and other threshold amounts to dodge Softwares and prevent banks from filing CTRs and STRs. These deposits are also routed through numerous accounts in multiple banks for this purpose.

All this jugglery takes some time and the company's valuation soars to new heights.

After say one year, the Balance Sheet of Farce Limited becomes stronger as follows:

Farce Limited

Liabilities	Amount (INR)	Assets	Amount (INR)
Equity			
Share Capital 510,000 of INR 10 each	5,100,000	Fixed Assets	2,000,000
Reserves and Surplus		Cash-in-Hand, Bank Account and Investments	7,600,000
Profit and Loss Account	5,000,000		
Current Liabilities	500,000	Other Current Assets including Loans and Advances	1,000,000
Total	**10,600,000**	**Total**	**10,600,000**

As seen from above, the Profit and Loss Account has jumped from INR 1 Mio to INR 5 Mio.

At this point of time, M/s Jockey & Co. decides to buy Darkhorse's stake back from him.

Jockey tries to pretend that he made a big mistake by selling 1.96% stake in a great start-up company to Darkhorse at such a low price and offers to buy-back all 10,000 shares of Darkhorse at INR 1 Mio regrettably i.e. at the asking price of INR 100 per share. Darkhorse laughingly agrees to the proposal. Remember Darkhorse bought them at INR 10 per share.

Darkhorse gets a cheque of INR 1 Mio (10,000 shares x INR 100) from M/s Jockey & Co. and he simultaneously, hands over his black money of INR 1 Mio (plus commission) to Jockey. Money Laundered.

Darkhorse keeps INR 0.90 Mio as Capital Gains Profit (White Money) on which he will pay applicable taxes. In case, he decides to lower his tax liability in this laundering, he would sell shares in Farce only after a period of 2 years post which his Long Term Capital Gain is taxable at lower rate.

In case any reader observed that the profit of Farce has increased to 5x whereas Jockey is willing to buy shares from Darkhorse at 10x its original price; kindly note that potential of growth is valued differently by different set of investors and only Jockey knows the true potential of Farce Limited. Start-Ups these days are valued more than many blue chip companies.

Scenario 2: Farce is a small listed company:

In case Farce Limited is a small company listed on a Stock Exchange, M/s Jockey & Co. would use Circular Trading (we discussed this method in our Penny Stock chapter) to inflate the share price of Farce Limited to INR 100 or above.

M/s Jockey & Co. would take their own sweet time of at least one year to inflate the price post which the LTCGs in the hands of Darkhorse are exempt from taxation.

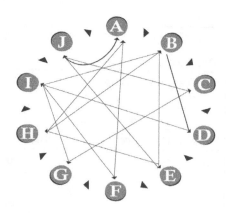

A Web Of Criss-Cross Transactions Between Brokers

PS: *Capital Gains from sale of shares in an unlisted company are considered as Long Term after 2 years whereas this period reduces to one year in case of listed companies if the sale-purchase is done through a Stock Exchange. Long Term Capital Gains (LTCG) on listed shares are exempt from tax if Securities Transaction Tax (STT) thereon is paid which is generally the case if trading happens over stock exchange. STT is a nominal tax on trading of securities ranging from 0.01% to 0.125% for shares. LTCG on unlisted shares is not exempt but chargeable at low rate of taxation.*

At INR 100 per share, Jockey & Co. buys his 10,000 shares back from Darkhorse in white money. Darkhorse gets cheque of INR 1 Mio for the sale and Jockey gets INR 1 Mio (plus his commission) in black money. Effect is the same - money laundered and that too without tax in this case.

POINTS TO PONDER:

$ Although everything seems legal with respect to Darkhorse's transactions above but with the advent of Companies Act 2013, the application of this method has got a big blow. This new Companies Act has restricted the number of investors in a private placement offer to a maximum of 50 at a time and maximum of 200 in aggregate in any Financial Year subject to several other terms and conditions.

$ Further, as per the draft rules under Companies Act, investors to whom shares/securities have been allotted under private placement route cannot transfer it to more than a certain number of people.

METHOD 24

Issuance of Shares to the Marginalised

There are many people in the country who are marginalised and poor and therefore do not share any responsibility towards payment of Income Tax. These people can be unskilled or semi-skilled workers like labourers, slum dwellers, scavengers, artisans, drivers, maids, cooks, servants etc. Even non-earning members of own family are used for Money Laundering purpose under this method.

The modus operandi

Darkhorse wants to convert INR 5 Mio of his black money into white. He with the help of Jockey has incorporated a company – Farce Private Ltd. for the purpose.

The Balance Sheet of Farce Private Limited on a given date is as follows:

Farce Private Limited

Liabilities	Amount(INR)	Assets	Amount(INR)
Equity		Assets	
Share Capital	100,000,000	Fixed Assets,	110,000,000
10,000,000 shares of INR 10 each		Bank Accounts, Investments etc.	
Surplus Reserves	10,000,000		
Profit and Loss Account			
Total	**110,000,000**	**Total**	**110,000,000**

Darkhorse and family owns 100% share capital in Farce Limited. Farce Limited is generally Shell Company with no or negligible business and works as a front company for Money Laundering purposes. Accordingly it has some profit in its reserves.

Now 200 poor and illiterate people are contacted. Their Permanent Account Numbers (PAN) / Income Tax Identifications are duly arranged and Bank Accounts opened in their name.

Darkhorse hands over INR 25,000 to each of these 200 people (along with their commission) and asks them to deposit the same in their bank accounts. They are then made to sign the share application form which states that they are applying to 2500 shares each in Farce Private Limited at Face Value of INR 10/- each. Signing fees to sign documents is paid to them additionally.

All 200 people likewise apply for 2500 shares each and issue cheques or wire transfer INR 25,000 in the bank account of the company. Farce issues fresh share capital of INR 5,000,000 (2500 shares x INR 10 Face Value x 200 people) to these people.

Darkhorse has received INR 5 Mio of white money in the company which he controls. Money Laundered tax free since the share capital issued by the company is not taxable in its hands.

Now the Balance Sheet of Farce Private Limited looks like following:

Farce Private Limited

Liabilities	Amount(INR)	Assets	Amount(INR)
Equity		Assets	
Share Capital 10,500,000 shares of INR 10 each	105,000,000	Fixed Assets, Bank Accounts, Investments etc. (Existing) + INR 5 Mio (Addition)	115,000,000
Surplus Reserves Profit and Loss Account	10,000,000		
Total	**115,000,000**	**Total**	**115,000,000**

Please note that shares issued by the company have been allotted at INR 10 each which is less than their Fair Value of INR 11 each and thus seemingly justifiable.

Jockey, the entry operator receives commission for laundering huge sums of black money for Darkhorse. Besides other formalities, he also files Income Tax Returns of the 200 share subscribers by showing Income of approximately INR 100,000 - 200,000 each from taxi fare, tuition fees, meal distribution, tailoring, weaving, washing, cooking, waste collecting etc. Their income stated above is not taxable being lower than the threshold amount and if ever required by tax officials, they explain that the INR 25,000 of cash deposit in their accounts was out of the aforementioned income and past savings.

Although shareholding of Darkhorse gets diluted by 4.76% (0.50 Mio shares ÷ 10.50 Mio shares) from 100% in this example, he is careful enough to keep blank share transfer deeds with himself which have already been signed by these poor people. The share certificates are handed over to these people only if they are summoned by Income Tax Department so that they can produce it as a proof of their genuine investment.

In reality, there can be larger number of people and larger amount than INR 25000/- each.

POINTS TO PONDER:

$ If infusion of capital in the aforesaid manner becomes difficult due to stringent regulations applicable over private placement of shares, a new company was formed in the same manner as stated in this method to bypass those regulations.

$ Revisions to Income Tax Act 1961 has given a big blow to this method by putting the burden of proof on the closely held company to prove that the amount received from shareholders as mentioned above belongs to them. In case, the Assessing Officer of Income Tax Department is not satisfied, the company will have to pay tax on this kind of fresh equity infusion.

$ The law even states that in case the poor subscribers mentioned above are not able to prove the source of their income to the satisfaction of Tax Officer, they will taxed at the highest rate of 30.9% on their declared income even if it is lower than the threshold amount of taxation. The method of tracing them and recovering tax from them is however not properly laid out.

METHOD 25

Trade Based Money Laundering (TBML): A New Approach to Money Laundering

Money Laundering has always existed and will always exist in a world of controls. It has been continuing since ages and it will continue to exist till we move to a world where people are free to do anything they want to do to earn money with no restriction and no taxation and still there being no crime and corruption. Moreover, all these good things must also exist at par across all jurisdictions of the globe. If you think, such a world is just a fancy equilibrium then equally fancy is the thought that there will be a definite end to Money Laundering. Absence of such equilibrium in this commercial world is the whole edifice of Black Money and Money Laundering.

Money Laundering emanated centuries ago from restrictions on alcohol and drugs which continue till date leading to a shadow economy of these goods as well as laundering of money. As the restrictions expanded from one commodity to another, one geography to another; ways got created to circumvent such barriers that restrict making money.

For example: If there is an entry barrier in form of higher import duty on a particular commodity, TBML will take place in form of Under-Invoicing of such goods wherein that commodity having an actual value of INR 100 will be shipped at a price say INR 90 so that the effect of higher import duty is off-set. Balance INR 10 will be paid to the exporter through Hawala (Informal Remittance System). Will Customs Department be able to distinguish between the same commodity priced at INR 100 and INR 90 is more of a rhetorical question.

Incredulous majority of Money Laundering takes place through international trade because people in the ML industry know that keeping money abroad is the safest mode of stashing illicit wealth. Any amount of money can be remitted anywhere in the world via wire transfer. It can be sent outside a country and brought back inside as and when required through TBML. Use of credit facilities like Bank Guarantee (BG)/ Standby Letter of Credit (SBLC) and Letters of Credit (LC) from banks besides wire transfer system gives a legitimate look to the entire Money Laundering transaction.

TBML is also a big reason that Demonetisation of currency notes in India will have less impact on ML since it does not gives not much significance to cash.

Use of LC in TBML:

To make the Money Laundering transactions appear more genuine, the parties include a LC in between.

Letter of Credit is a document from a bank guaranteeing that a seller will receive payment in full as long as the delivery conditions written on the trade documents have been met. In the event that the buyer is unable to make payment on the purchase, the bank will pay the outstanding amount.

Example:

There are two parties in two different countries - Mr J in Japan and Mr I in India. J is a manufacturer of certain raw materials that are required by I in India for his manufacturing unit. I approaches J to purchase the goods he manufactures. J agrees to sell but wants entire payment upfront as he does not want to take risk of non-payment by I when the goods reach India. I on the other hand does not want to make any significant payment upfront as he is not sure if J will deliver the goods of right quality at right time after receiving full payment.

It means that both of them being located in different countries are not very comfortable in taking risk on each other. To sort out the problems like this in an international trade, a LC is used. In this situation; I goes to Bank of India of which he is a good customer and gets an LC issued in favour of J of Japan. The LC states that in case, I is not able to pay the required amount to J, Bank of India will pay to him as long as the delivery conditions are met. Bank of India, thus guarantees payment to J on behalf of I.

After Bank of India has agreed to furnish the LC on behalf of I, another problem may come up in form of J's lack of confidence over Bank of India. In such case, he will rope in a bank of Japan say Bank of Tokyo on which he can rely upon. Now, the LC issued by Bank of India (LC issuing bank) will be confirmed by Bank of Tokyo (Confirming Bank). The confirming bank guarantees the payment to J in case the LC issuing bank defaults.

The trade can be done now and J can very well export the goods to I even on credit (technically called usance) of few months.

The difference between a BG and a LC is that a Letter of Credit is solely based upon the completion and accuracy of documents known as a *'complying presentation'* which means that if the conditions stated in the LC are fully complied, it must be honoured irrespective of everything else. Banks bind themselves by the terms of the LC. If these terms have been accepted by the parties, Bank is not bothered with what happens in the actual transaction. In Bank Guarantee, there is no such condition of complying presentation of documents and the issuing bank is liable to pay unconditionally without any demur whenever a claim has been made.

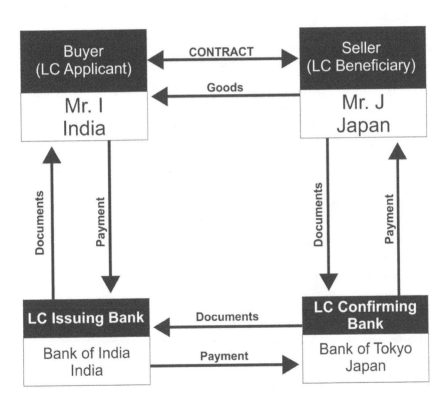

An invoice is the most important document in trade not only because it transfers the title of goods but also because it specifies and to an extent certifies the value of goods or services sold. And the trick of the game here is that no one knows whether the value stated in the invoice is the true value of such goods and services.

Over-Invoicing and Under-Invoicing are the two prominent ways in which TBML works. They are time tested modus operandi for circulating and laundering of black money:

METHODS USED IN TBML:

Method 25.1: Over-Invoicing

Mr Darkhorse has USD 1 Million of Black Money in his company's bank accounts. He has got sufficient money for his needs and luxuries in India but is afraid that his black money may get caught by the government here. He therefore thinks of remitting his No. 2 Money (Black Money) outside India mixed with some legitimate transaction.

Darkhorse approaches his friend Jockey who is a member of a global Money Laundering cartel and both of them agree to take the government system for a ride.

Jockey introduces Darkhorse to Mr Whitehorse. Whitehorse is in the business of manufacturing some auto components. He orders a machine from Mr Fairhorse (another affiliate of Jockey) in Indonesia whose actual price is USD 5 Mio but Fairhorse invoices it to him at USD 6.20 Mio with a package of Technical and Installation Fees as well as Extended Warranty for two years so as to make the price look extremely authentic.

Whitehorse pays USD 6.20 Mio to Fairhorse of Indonesia. Fairhorse keeps USD 5.20 Mio with himself as price of machine (USD 5 Mio) plus his commission for facilitating the transaction (USD 0.20 Mio) and remits USD 1 Mio as per the instruction from Jockey to a HR Robo company in Hong Kong in lieu of some Human Resources consultancy through a robotics software. This company is directly or indirectly controlled by Darkhorse.

Thus, settlements on both sides happen through bogus trades. In India, Darkhorse transfers his black money to Whitehorse by buying some (fictitious) goods and services from Darkhorse totalling USD 1 Mio. In Indonesia, Black Money is transferred from Fairhorse to Darkhorse in garb of consultancy fees paid to some offshore entity in Hong Kong which is controlled by Darkhorse through unknown bearer shares.

Over Invoicing

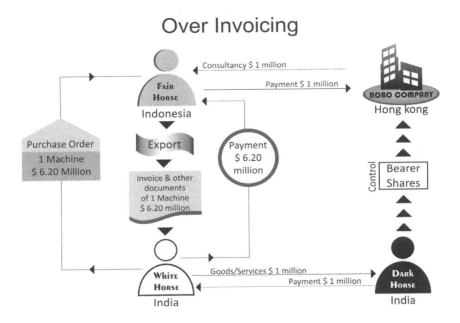

In real scenarios, lot of layers and complexity is added to the transaction. It may happen that the goods are coming from Indonesia directly but the trade is being facilitated by some Jockey in Hong Kong so that money goes to Hong Kong which is a trade hub and bank secrecy laws are in place.

Method 25.2: Under-Invoicing

Cocaine (a prohibited narcotic) of USD 1 Mio was imported into India or is planned to be imported into India at a later date. Darkhorse in India wants to send USD 1 Mio to Hong Kong as payment for these drugs. The payment is facilitated through Under-Invoicing.

Jockey in Hong Kong starts the process. He orders auto components from Darkhorse for USD 5 Mio. Actual value of these components is USD 6 Mio as per their secret agreement/ understanding.

Upon receipt of the Purchase Order, Darkhorse ships the components to Jockey in Hong Kong who then remits this amount to Darkhorse. Jockey sells these goods either domestically or internationally through exports and realizes it's FMV of INR 6 Mio. He transfers the excess money of USD 1 Mio to the drug cartel after keeping a conversion commission for himself.

Under Invoicing

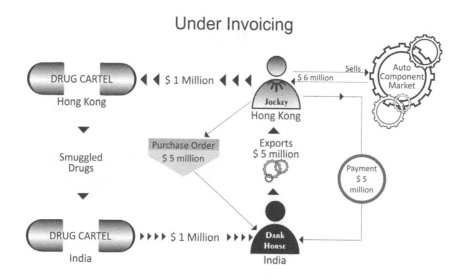

In the example above, there was export of goods from India and outward remittance from Hong Kong since the party in India illegally imported prohibited goods and paid for that in a seemingly legal way. Under-Invoicing can take place in opposite direction also without involving banned goods.

Example: Darkhorse in India wants to send USD 1 Mio to Hong Kong as he wants to stash some of his black money abroad. He has a trusted accountant in the form of Jockey in Hong Kong who keeps his black money safe in the bank accounts of some shell companies spread over various countries. In this case:

Jockey orders USD 5 Mio of Auto Components from Darkhorse. Actual value of these components is USD 6 Mio as per their secret agreement/ understanding. Darkhorse ships the components to Jockey in Hong Kong who then remits USD 5 Mio to Darkhorse. Jockey sells these goods for USD 6 Mio and transfers excess money as per the instruction from Darkhorse after deducting a commission for himself. The transfer of USD 1 Mio will be in the garb of consultancy services received by some companies in offshore jurisdictions whose ultimate beneficial owner is Darkhorse. Money Laundered.

In domestic trade, it requires no big expertise to misprice a commodity on invoice and other documents but since the black money needs to be circulated overseas, the real Money Laundering game is played in international trade. Some of the ways/methods in which Over-Invoicing and Under-Invoicing is done in international trade is as under:

1. **False Value of Goods:** A USD 100 value item is simply stated at USD 105 or USD 95 in the trade documents and humongous amounts get laundered

through large quantities and numerous rounds of trade. Although Customs Department of every country knows the value of every good as per the HS code from Harmonised System of Classification of Goods given by world customs, it is not difficult to marginally increase or decrease the price of goods in trade documents. Further this harmonised system is also not beneficial when it comes to trading of intangible goods and services.

2. **False Description of Goods:** Use of goods that resemble each other but have different values or goods whose nomenclature resembles but have different values. The documents of these goods can be misguiding with respect to their price. For example: Black Shoe (INR 5000/- per pair) and Shoe Black – Polish (INR 50 per piece) may be written in trade documents interchangeably whereas trade may be of either shoes or polish resulting in extreme over/under pricing.

|INR 5000| |INR 50|

An importer and exporter has no restriction to trade in any specific commodity. He can trade in any commodity in international markets where he finds opportunity to make money and therefore he can choose any commodity where he finds scope for laundering of black money. Many times the IEC (Importer Exporter Code) Number is obtained in the name of illiterate people who are unaware of the whole scheme and are paid money to sign few documents.

3. **Over or Under Shipment:** The quantity of trade as mentioned in the documents can be different from the actual quantity. Example: Documents prepared for 3000 pashmina (a fine variety of wool) shawls whereas the container has only 2200 pashmina shawls mixed with 800 low value similar looking shawls. All 3000 shawls bear similar colours and have same individual packing.

Another example is ink pens where normal ink pens may be mixed with gold nib ink pens. Similarly, there can be actual luxury watches mixed with 1st copy watches. In one case, gold was smuggled into a country in form of small nuts and bolts which were coated with a moulding of nickel and brass. On melting, nickel and brass got separated from gold.

4. **Star/Status Exporters and Importers:** Importers and Exporters who are status holders need to give a self-declaration only for importing/exporting the goods. Their customs clearance is fast tracked and these trading houses do big volumes of shipments on daily basis. Inspectors of these traders do not ask many questions while giving out inspection certificates and are paid for their services by traders. Ironically presence of all these factors is ripe for Money Laundering and therefore money launderers approach these traders for fulfilment of their illicit purposes.

5. **Dual Use Goods:** Some goods have dual use and they are permitted for trade in one form/use but restricted in another form. Example: Import of new cars is permitted in India but import of used cars is restricted. Thus, a used car becomes a new car in trade documents where it is priced higher to disguise the customs. Similarly there are various chemicals, drugs and medicines that have difficult nomenclature and their restricted form is not specified verbatim in the trade documents to disguise people.

6. **Rejected/ Waste Goods:** Many high value goods are disguised as rejected goods to lower the import duty. This slyness also happens when there is restriction on import of certain goods in one form or another. In such a case they are traded in form of rejected or waste material. Many goods get useless on a slight defect and such a defect may not be visible apparently. Example: Shoes in a pair whose size don't match only slightly or garments where just a stitch is inferior or missing etc. Such defects render the whole item worthless or reduce its value to scrap without getting detected by customs or government inspectors.

| USD 100 | USD 10 | USD 50 | USD 5 |

7. **Difficult to value goods and services:** Many items make their valuers go crazy. Best example of such a commodity is diamond. Since it is difficult to value them, TBML goes rampantly in diamonds. Another example is intangible goods like computer softwares. Different anti-virus programmes can command different values and similarly, services are difficult to value too. Different clients can assign different values for the same advice. Then

there is 'Art Work' where beauty lies in the eyes of the beholder. Toys, Luxury Watches, Mobile Handsets and Electronic Goods are all gullible to mispricing. Who can tell whether a Doll is worth $10 or $20?

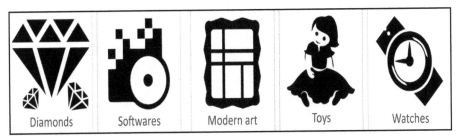

| Diamonds | Softwares | Modern art | Toys | Watches |

8. **Phantom Shipping:** Phantom shipping means empty shipping. Thus, it is an over pricing tool. Here trade and transport documents are all prepared immaculately but there is no actual transport of goods. The respective container may be either empty or contains sand equal to the weight stated in documents. The reason behind use of phantom shipping is that Banks while processing a trade transaction (either with or without LC) focus only on complying presentation of the documents and if they are in order, they do not worry about petty things like phantom shipping.⊠ Please note that inspection certificate and customs clearance do form part of these documents but parties to trade are experts in arranging them through informal ways.

It may be noted that Government of India and many other countries provide monetary incentive to promote exports. These can be in form of excise and customs Duty Drawback on exports of goods from the country. So if a trader exports certain goods after incurring excise duty (levied on manufacture of these goods) or customs duty (levied on import of these goods), he will be paid a large portion of the such duties back (say 95%) in form of export incentives. In addition, government pays a fixed percentage (say 5%) of the export value of goods to these exporters. Thus, traders can falsely claim higher Duty Drawback from government by over-invoicing their exports.

A brief snapshot of Over-Invoicing and Under-Invoicing (mispricing) and its misuse is as follows:

Over-Invoicing:	**Signifies:**
	Actual Value of Goods: INR 100
	Value in Invoice and Trade Documents: INR 110
Over-invoicing of exports from India:	**Purpose/Use:**
	Bringing black money into India from overseas.
	Settlement of a previous TBML or Hawala Transaction
	Higher Duty Drawback (Export Incentive) from government.
	Higher Revenue in Books of Accounts leading to higher credit limits from banks or lower cost of funding from them.
	A commission (conversion charge) to facilitate the transaction in case it is done for a third party.
Over-invoicing of imports into India:	**Purpose/Use:**
	Stashing of black money abroad
	Settlement of a previous TBML or Hawala Transaction
	Higher Cost of Purchases to avoid taxes.
	A commission (conversion charge) to facilitate the transaction in case it is done for a third party.
Under-invoicing:	**Signifies:**
	Actual Value of Goods: INR 100
	Value in Invoice and Trade Documents: INR 90
Under-invoicing of exports from India:	**Purpose/Use:**
	Stashing of black money abroad
	Settlement of a previous TBML or Hawala Transaction
	Lower Customs Duty in India (if applicable on exports)
	Lower Customs Duty (on imports) in foreign jurisdiction
	Lower Revenue in Books of Accounts to avoid taxes.
	A commission (conversion charge) to facilitate the transaction in case it is done for a third party.
Under-invoicing of imports into India:	**Purpose/Use:**
	Bringing black money into India from overseas.
	Settlement of a previous TBML or Hawala Transaction
	Lower Customs Duty in India (on imports)
	Lower Customs Duty in foreign jurisdiction (if applicable on exports)
	Lower Purchase Cost in Books of Accounts and thus higher operating margin to please banks and other analysts.
	A commission (conversion charge) to facilitate the transaction in case it is done for a third party.

Method 25.3: LC Bill Discounting (Accommodation I)

Darkhorse and Whitehorse, both are good friends and both are businessmen. They run their businesses by availing cheap finance from banks arranged through LC Bill Discounting (LCBD). The method is also known as Accommodation Bill. Although it mostly happens in domestic sales but its use in international trade (imports and exports) cannot be ruled out.

The modus operandi:

Darkhorse needs low cost finance of INR 100.

He sells goods to Whitehorse for INR 125 with a credit (usance) of three months.

Whitehorse who is the buyer/importer in this case opens an LC from Bank of India (BOI) in favour of Darkhorse for INR 125 for a period of three months. *(PS: Both Darkhorse and Whitehorse are good enough customers of banks to avail LC limits)*

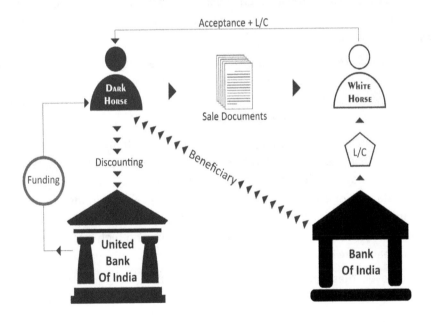

Darkhorse accepts the documents sent by Whitehorse which implies acceptance to his liability to pay Whitehorse a sum of INR 125 after a period of three months.

Darkhorse discounts the sale bills from United Bank of India (UBI) and gets INR 120 as LCBD Finance. The rate of interest is minimal since the discounting is based upon the strength of LC from Bank (BOI) that has guaranteed the payment.

After 3 months, Whitehorse pays to Darkhorse and Darkhorse settles the loan with UBI. Whitehorse can pay directly to UBI also.

This is the most rampant form of Money Laundering which is structured only to obtain low cost funds from Bank and utilize it in riskier businesses where return on money is higher.

The catch here is that there may be no movement of actual goods. Since LC is based solely upon documents, the documents are prepared to the satisfaction of bankers who are not bothered to check the actual movement of goods. The transport documents – Lorry /Goods Receipt /AWB (Air Way Bill) /B/L (Bill of Lading) which are presented to them as proof of shipment are prone to manipulation.

Since the scheme is mostly used in domestic trade, the Lorry Receipt or Goods Receipt that is given by a road transport (truck) company in most of these cases is easy to arrange for the parties.

The LC may even contain clauses like – All discrepancies are acceptable, third party payment is acceptable, any vehicle is acceptable, on-site inspection is waived etc. Both parties agree to these terms with equal vigour as they minimize any hindrance to this fabricated trade from banks.

The scheme is thus only a ploy to raise cheap finance from banks. It amounts to fake sales in many cases backed by fake purchases. These fake purchases are made in the similar way so as to facilitate finance to the other party who was a purchaser in first instance. For example: Darkhorse after availing low cost funds with the help of Whitehorse will now become a purchaser of goods from Whitehorse and help him in raising such low cost funds. They may be earning high rate of interest by funding real estate industry.

Moreover, these businessmen work in a cartel to use this instrument for continuously raising low cost funds from banks by issuing sale bills on each other.

Method 25.4: Export Finance (Accommodation II)

Similar to LCBD, Export Finance can also be (mis)used by traders to raise cheap finance from Banks and then divert the funds to a higher risk higher return business.

In India, export finance is provided by banks at extremely low rate of interest because all banks have targets for Priority Sector Lending (PSL) and Export Finance is treated as one of the priority sectors. Accordingly, it makes sense for banks to give loans at lower rate of interest to meet their PSL targets. Besides this, RBI gives an interest subvention of approximately 3% p.a. to Small Scale Industries on their export finance in INR. It means if an eligible borrower raises Export Finance from a Bank in INR at 9% p.a., it will receive an interest subsidy @3% p.a. from RBI and thus its effective cost of borrowing will be only 6% p.a.

Export Credit can be availed by a borrower prior to shipment (on showing the export order) and after shipment (on showing the invoice, shipping bill and other export documents). Pre-shipment finance (also known as Packing Credit) is generally restricted to a ballpark 75% of the Export Order but the borrower is well entitled to receive balance 25% of the export order after shipment of the goods.

In India, Export Credit (Pre-Shipment and Post-Shipment finance) is provided to an exporter for a maximum of 360 days but if it is availed by them for a period up to 180 days, the interest rate is even lower. Reason for this is not just tenor premium but also refinancing of export credit from RBI which is allowed up to a maximum of 180 days.

Now let us look at the modus operandi used to exploit the scheme:

The modus operandi:

1. WH is a trader (importer and exporter) and has its subsidiaries or affiliates in few countries for trading.

2. WH needs INR 200 for lending to sensitive sectors like Real Estate, Capital Markets, and Commodity Market etc. so as to earn high interest income from them.

3. WH decides to export INR 100 worth of goods to its subsidiary - JK in Dubai by over-invoicing them at INR 200. It therefore receives an export order of INR 200 from JK for the purpose.

4. WH avails Export Packing Credit (EPC) or pre-shipment finance of INR 150 (75% x INR 200 of Export Order) from BOI at 10% p.a. for 180 days as against its true eligibility of only INR 75 (75% x INR 100 of Actual Export Value). WH also gets interest subsidy of 3% from RBI against EPC. Its effective cost therefore comes to 7% p.a.

5. WH transfers this amount (INR 150) to one of its supplier (or route it through many suppliers) who in turn lends it to Real Estate Industry at 14% p.a. for 180 days. *(Layering keeps the transaction hidden in financial statements).*

6. WH exports the goods to JK after a period of 2 months/60 days and avails post-shipment credit for the balance amount i.e. INR 50 (25% x INR 200 of Export

Order) from BOI at 10% p.a. for 120 days as against its true eligibility of only INR 25 (25% x INR 100 of Actual Export Value).

WH transfers this amount (INR 50) again to Real Estate Industry through a bunch of its trusted suppliers at same rate of interest i.e. 14% p.a. for 120 days.

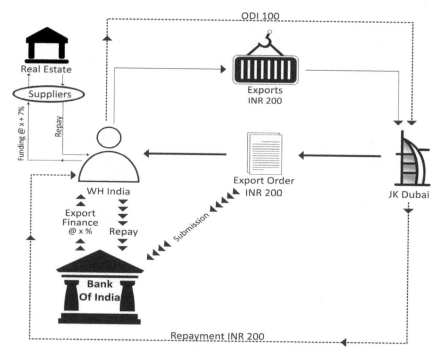

7. After 180 days from the date of shipment, the transactions are settled. WH receives the amount back from Real Estate players through its suppliers along with interest and returns the money back to the Bank.

8. *In effect, WH earned interest @ 7% p.a. (14% - 7%) through this scheme from diversion of funds which is otherwise not permitted as hence gives rise to his black money. This interest income will not be reflected in its books of account in its true form and will be priced in certain goods received from its hand in glove suppliers. This scheme may go on running continuously through continuous exports by WH who would be availing a running account export credit facility from the banks for the purpose.*

The other side of the story goes as under:

9. JK – the Dubai based subsidiary of WH faces difficulty in paying for the export order to WH since the goods received are worth only INR 100 whereas JK has to pay INR 200 to WH.

10. JK sells these goods in the market at say INR 110 and therefore books a loss in its books of accounts to the tune INR 90 (INR 200 purchase price – INR 110 sale price).

11. Now WH transfers funds to JK. WH remits INR 100 to JK as investment through ODI (Overseas Direct Investment) route under which companies are permitted to remit fund overseas for investment up to four times their net worth. Use of Hawala Route too cannot be ruled out.

12. Another option in case WH does not want to remit funds immediately is issuance of SBLC. WH issues a SBLC (Standby LC) i.e. a BG in favour of JK and JK raises loan from a bank in Dubai based on the strength of this SBLC/BG.

13. JK has now got INR 210 in its bank account (INR 100 received as Investment or Loan and INR 110 from sale of goods). JK remits INR 200 back to WH and settles the outstanding. Transaction complete.

In reality, since export finance can be refinanced by banks from RBI up to 180 days, WH will exploit the scheme only up to this period to keep the banks happy although it is allowed to realize the export proceeds from JK up to 360 days from the date of shipment.

The modus operandi stated above is over-simplification of the actual process which in reality will be far more complex and involve various parties acting in a cartel. It is an open tap of cheap finance to the traders and can lead to humungous amounts of diversion of funds.

Method 25.5: Import Finance (Accommodation III)

Like export finance helps exporters, import finance helps importers raise low cost funds from the banks. The instruments used here are Buyer's Credit and Supplier's Credit. Both these bank products extend the usance or credit period provided by the exporter to the importer thereby reducing importer's normal working capital cycle.

Example:

DH in India imports goods worth USD 100 from WH in Japan. The import is backed by LC from BOI with a usance period of three months. It means after three months from the date of shipment, DH will pay to the BOI which in turn will pay to WH in Japan.

Now DH avails a Buyer's Credit facility for one year for this transaction from an offshore branch of BOI or a Foreign Bank located out of India which is ready to lend to DH because of its credit worthiness. In such case, the payment of LC to BOI after three months is made by DH from the funds raised under the Buyer's Credit facility. His liability got extended by further twelve months at very low rate of interest.

Similarly WH, the exporter in Japan can also arrange cheap funds for DH from his Bank via Supplier's Credit for a period of one year. The result being the same, liability of DH extends by one year.

In India, RBI has tried to plug this tap of cheap funding by prescribing that the tenor of such loans to importers should not exceed their operating cycle less credit (usance) period offered to them by the exporters.

Period of Operating cycle can be easily computed by the following formula:

$$\frac{[\text{Inventory} + \text{Account Receivables} - \text{Account Payables}] \times 12}{\text{Annual Sales}}$$

Method 25.6: Merchanting Trade

Like LCBD is used as an Accommodation Entry mostly in domestic trade, Merchanting Trade is mis-utilized in international trade. Here the importer of goods exports them directly to a third country without bringing them into his country first. The criminality remains the same – suspicion over the movement of actual goods.

The modus operandi:

Merchanting Trade means that Mr X in India imports goods from Dubai and ships them directly to Singapore from Dubai without bringing them into India.

While all the regulatory requirements related to foreign exchange inward remittance from Singapore and outward remittance to Dubai and shall be fully met, the catch here is that no one knows what has actually been shipped from Dubai to Singapore. It can be anything from just nothing to any kind of prohibited goods including arms and ammunition.

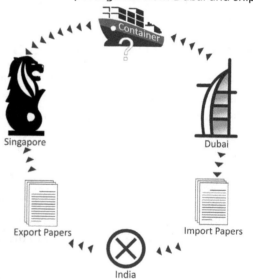

Besides, fake sales and purchase entry (accommodation), the method has enough potential to move huge sums of money from one country to another when it is clubbed with Over and Under-Invoicing.

Method 25.7: High Sea Sales

High Sea refers to a location that is beyond the territorial limits of the country. Therefore in case of India, High Sea Sales (HSS) mean sale of goods while they are in transit to India and before they reach the territorial limits of India.

For example: X in India imported medicines from Germany and before the consignment could reach Indian Territory, X found a buyer of these medicines in Y of India. He sold the goods to Y through a HSS Agreement. Now Y will get the goods cleared from customs and obtain the Bill of Entry. Payment to the exporter in Germany could be made by either X or Y.

In case X does not want to reveal the identity of the exporter, he will make the payment to exporter himself after obtaining the amount from Y else he may ask Y to make the payment directly to the exporter.

Major benefit of HSS is that X will not be liable to pay Sales Tax/VAT/GST on the HSS made to Y which he would have paid had he imported the goods into India first and then sold them to Y.

HSS, because of its low FOREX regulations can also become a facilitator of Money Laundering. Let us see how.

The modus operandi:

X who is an importer in India knows that the goods being imported by him are of inferior quality or say over invoiced. Therefore if he gets caught in any bad news, he may suffer a major loss. He therefore sells these goods as HSS to a company engaged in Money Laundering activities that provides such kind of reputational risk cover. Say X sells these goods to M/s Jockey & Co. who will then get the goods cleared from customs.

Depending upon their secret understanding; Jockey & Co. may make the payment to exporter directly and sell the goods back to X at a later date or sell them to a third party as per the instructions from X.

Method 25.8: Remittance of Export Claims (Defective Goods)

Exports made. Payment received. Now the importer claims certain goods to be defective and wants his payment of such goods back. Therefore remittance for such claims needs to be made if business relations with the importer need to be maintained.

However, remittance of Export Claims is a full-fledged method in itself for stashing of wealth overseas without any assistance from Over-Invoicing and Under-Invoicing.

The modus operandi:

Darkhorse in India exported goods worth USD 400,000 to Whitehorse in Malaysia. Payment is received in time. Now after sometime, Whitehorse claims 5% of the goods to be defective and therefore he needs his money back for the defective goods of USD 20,000. Darkhorse agrees and approaches his bank to remit this amount to Whitehorse.

Banks will be happy to remit this small amount after simply checking the FIRC (Foreign Inward Remittance Certificate) issued for the export proceeds received by him at the first instance. After getting satisfied from FIRC that Darkhorse has already received full payment for exports, they agree to return this small amount of USD 20,000. They will earn a good FOREX margin on the remittance and will never get suspicious of such a small amount of sales return.

This is the whole edifice of this modus operandi. Fill an ocean, drop by drop. Many such payments will be made on account of defective goods from multiple banks.

In this scheme, Whitehorse may either be hand in glove with Darkhorse or he may be a sole selling / commission agent of Darkhorse who sells his goods to multiple importers in Malaysia, in which case, his prospects to lodge claim for defective goods are higher.

The amount so remitted to Whitehorse is transferred to an overseas shell corporation by showing some contractual income in favour of that company. Needless to state, such company would be under control of Darkhorse. Money Laundered.

The other illegitimate benefit which Darkhorse might try to get through this scheme is Export Incentive. Technically, he should return/ reverse the Duty Drawback amount received from government on USD 20,000 of defective goods but he may try to withhold this amount by conniving with the auditors.

Method 25.9: Export of goods as Sample

Samples are not meant for sale. But who knows if that is actually the case.

Export of goods as sample play the role of a gift in a scheme of Money Laundering. Since these goods are going out of India to be distributed for free, neither they are likely to return to India, nor is any money from their sales is expected. An excellent scheme for stashing money abroad which can send shivers down the spine when coupled with Under-Invoicing.

The modus operandi:

Darkhorse while going abroad takes some of his goods with himself as samples which are otherwise not intended for sale. He however sells these goods abroad and deposits the money in his offshore accounts. He comes back to India and is not required to explain the use of his goods.

However, there is a restriction in place with respect to the amount of samples that can be distributed overseas annually. Darkhorse therefore chooses to fill his ocean drop by drop by selling his samples within this limit.

The other way of exploiting this method is by clubbing it with Under-Invoicing. Suppose the statutory limit for Darkhorse to take his samples out of India is USD 1 Million and he under-invoices the value of his samples by 3x which means he can now take out goods worth USD 3 Mio, sell them and stash the money out of the country.

Method 25.10: Write-Off of Export Receivables

Write off of Export Receivables is actually a loss to the exporter but if it is pre-planned, it is his gain. Confused! Well, here's the Modus Operandi.

The modus operandi:

Darkhorse in India exports USD 100 worth of goods to his trading partner - Whitehorse in Dubai.

He subsequently informs his banker not to expect full amount to be received for this export. Darkhorse tells his bank that Whitehorse will only pay USD 90 for his goods, balance USD 10 needs to be written off as non-recoverable since some of the goods did not fully match his specifications.

We know however, that in reality Whitehorse will keep USD 10 as a custodian of Darkhorse to be transferred to some offshore shell corporation as per his instructions.

Now, unlike write-off of domestic receivables, writing off of export receivables has restrictions. It needs to be informed to the Authorised Dealer (Bank) of the customer which in turn informs to RBI. Further, the amount which can be written off in a year is capped, over which RBI's permission is required.

In this case, Darkhorse will be clever enough to write-off the amount only up to his permissible limit without escalating the matter up to RBI. See, drop by drop he fills his ocean.

What's more, he even gets tax benefit on the amount written off as non-recoverable which is a deductible expenditure under Indian Income Tax Act.

Method 25.11: Advance Remittance and Cancellation of Order

Advance Remittance is the money paid in advance by an importer to an exporter with respect to the goods he wants to import. Advance remittance can be made either by an Importer in India to an exporter in a foreign country or can be received by an exporter in India from an Importer in a foreign country. In both cases therefore, it can be used to send and receive Black Money in a pre-planned way.

What happens after advance remittance is the cancellation of the purchase order against which it was made.

Next, consequent to cancellation of purchase order, the amount paid/received as advance is forfeited. Money Laundered.

The modus operandi:

Darkhorse in India intends to buy some goods worth USD 1 Mio from Whitehorse in Hong Kong. He gives a purchase order for this purpose to Whitehorse.

Whitehorse asks for advance payment of 10%. Darkhorse remits USD 100,000 (10% of USD 1 Mio) to him.

After some time, Darkhorse decides that the goods he is buying from Whitehorse are not up to his specifications and expectation. He cancels his purchase order.

Whitehorse states he had started work on that purchase order and will incur loss if the order is cancelled. Whitehorse therefore forfeits the advance payment received. Money Laundered.

In reality both Darkhorse and Whitehorse are hand in glove. Whitehorse keeps USD 100,000 as a custodian of Darkhorse or will transfer it to some offshore shell corporation as per his instructions.

This scheme makes it easy to remit black money from one country to another without bothering for any shipment formalities.

Method 25.12: Multiple Accounts for imports

Every trader is not big enough to avail LC limits from a Bank on favourable terms like low commission rate, low margin requirement etc. Therefore many times, one big trader opens an LC to import few consignments on behalf of various small traders and those imports are then distributed among them.

This is a win-win way of doing business for both small as well as large traders but this method is prone to misuse. Let us see how:

The modus operandi:

Bank Accounts are opened in the names of 200 poor illiterate people who are paid to get their accounts opened in a Bank and sign few documents.

Cash is deposited in these 200 accounts taking due care of the regulatory thresholds to avoid CTR and STR reporting.

All the money is then transferred and pooled in a single account.

From this account, Foreign Exchange Outward Remittance is made to a company in overseas. The reasons cited to bankers can be a plenty:

✓ It could be sent as an Advance Remittance for certain exports on behalf of various importers.

✓ It could be sent as a full and final payment for goods already imported which are actually fake. Example: First copy of Original Branded Mobile Phones.

All the documents required for this trade are shown to the bankers to their satisfaction. Money Gone.

It will get stashed in the overseas accounts of the importer.

Method 25.13: Multiple Invoicing

This is a scheme to defraud the banks and bring back the Black Money illicitly stashed overseas. Preparing multiple invoices as against a single shipment of goods enables multiple inflows of Black Money into India.

The modus operandi:

Darkhorse exported a single consignment of goods to Whitehorse but made 5 Invoices of this shipment, four of which are just duplicates. These four duplicate invoices are certified from customs as originals by duping those officials.

Besides Invoices, banks also require Shipping Bill and Transport Documents (Airway Bill (AWB) or Bill of Lading (B/L) or Lorry Receipt) as proof of export. Duplicates of Shipping Bill and Transport Documents are easily received from Shipping / transport company by giving them commission and promising them more business in future. In many countries like USA, there is no requirement of a shipping bill which makes the process easier.

Now against a single shipment, five sets of documents are given to five different banks of which only one is original. Money flows in all these five bank accounts and all five are happy to charge FOREX margin on the inward remittances and earn fee based income. Money Laundered Four times (4x) the export amount.

Since launderers keep devising innovative means to launder money on a continuous basis, it can never be possible to prepare an exhaustive list of such ways. However, the methods stated above are some of the common and most prominent ones used in TBML. They flourish because of the laxity present in our system.

Reasons for flourishing TBML:

$ Income from trade transactions is a low risk, high return business for all banks. It therefore generates pressure from business side on AML and Trade Finance departments resulting in oversight of suspicious transactions.

$ Banks fear that making their customers uncomfortable by questioning them will shift their business to another bank.

$ In case of shell companies, money launderers elevate the profile of the directors of the company fictitiously by showing higher income of directors, filing their ITRs, paying nominal taxes and declaring various non-existing assets in their names. This prevents generation of Suspicious Transaction Alert by the banking software.

$ Even if suspicious transaction alert gets generated, not all of them are properly investigated by the bank officials resulting to oversight in filing of STRs with FIU of the government.

$ Further, banks are not supposed to stop a suspicious transaction because it will alert the money launderer who will then take his Money Laundering business to some other place or reshape the whole scheme.

$ The STRs coming from all the banks and all branches become a full truck load of documents for FIU that needs huge resources and infrastructure to process it diligently.

$ TBML may be going on right under the nose of bank officials and they may not be able to detect it because it lacks awareness.

$ TBML uses banking channels and credit facilities to its benefit. It uses wire transfers and bank products like LC, Bill Discounting etc. to its advantage. Many of the schemes explained above are bona fide ways to promote trade but they are being mis-utilized by money launderers.

$ In case of shell companies, there is no authentic way in which identity of beneficial owners can be established.

$ Banks do not have proper systems and models in place to deter TBML. The connection between the AML cell and the credit or marketing department of the Bank is not robust.

$ There is limited sharing of information on TBML between banks.

$ In case of foreign remittances, proper due diligence of foreign party is either:

✓ Not done

Or

✓ Not done through a capable agency to avoid costs

Or

✓ Contents of the due diligence report are not properly investigated.

For example: the Dun and Bradstreet (D&B) Report on a Hong Kong based company says: Company has one room office in XXX Building located on YY Street. One director namely Mr Whitehorse found but he is not having sufficient information about company's business model.

Banks instead of investigating this matter deeper are happy in just filing the report for compliance on paper.

$ The modi operandi stated in this chapter are over-simplified for understanding purposes. In real cases however, it is marred with complexity and every inch of the scheme is planned immaculately in advance. For example: there can be various modifications in the purchase order, dozens of complicated correspondence, amendments in the LC terms, single illegitimate transaction hidden under the robust past track record of hundreds of legitimate ones etc.

$ TBML falls under Operational Risk of banks, where models for measurement of risk are quite arbitrary to capture the AML risk. Moreover, the quantum of penalties levied by RBI for facilitating Money Laundering is on lower side.

$ Customs department is not well equipped to inspect all the goods taking part in international trade. They rely on the inspection certificate provided by traders and since the payment to inspecting agencies is made by the traders, they are bound to follow their paymasters. Customs on their own checks only 15%-20% of the all the shipments on a random basis and even the contents of those selected randomly is not checked in entirety.

As evident from above, banks have also become a party in facilitating the Money Laundering activities along with customs, FIU and other agencies for the want of appropriate action at the appropriate time.

POINTS TO PONDER:

$ Since TBML takes place through Banks, Banks have a huge responsibility to deter it. Banks need to question the genuineness and commercial sense of every transaction to prevent any ingenuity creep in.

$ Banks should do a profile check of all the parties behind a trade transaction to find out their capacity and credibility in executing that transaction.

$ The outlier transactions which do not appear to match the standard transactions are the ones with high probability of money laundering.

$ Details of suppliers and vendors can be called in case there are huge volumes of transactions with small number of traders and who are not well known.

$ RBI can levy bigger penalties for lax compliance of AML procedures and can stress upon the Banks to build scientific models to capture this risk.

METHOD 26

Taking Benefit of Special Economic Zones (SEZ)

SEZ/ Free Trade Zones (FTZ) are specially designated areas in a country created for the purpose of promoting trade, business and inflow of foreign exchange.

There can be different names given to these areas by different countries. They can be called FTZ, SEZ, Foreign Trade Zones, Export Processing Zones (EPZ), Enterprise Zones etc.

In India, they exist in form of SEZ and are regulated by SEZ Act 2005. The concept of SEZ is that it is a duty free enclave and is deemed to be a foreign territory for the purpose of trade operations.

Since they are considered to be foreign territory, the other part of the country is called Domestic Tariff Area (DTA) and the sales by units in SEZ to someone in DTA is considered as Exports and regulated likewise despite the fact that both SEZ and DTA are geographically located within the territories of the same country.

The units in SEZ are given various incentives to lure business houses and entrepreneurs to establish their manufacturing, processing or delivery units in the zone which will help a country increase its exports, earn foreign currency as well develop an otherwise unattractive region.

SEZ units are exempted from customs duty, excise duty, Sales Tax/VAT, Service Tax, Stamp Duty, Registration Fees, Electricity Duty etc. They are also exempted from payment of Income Tax either fully or partially for a certain number of years known as tax holiday. These incentives may differ from one country to another.

Although these monetary benefits are bestowed upon them by the government for bona fide reasons, many SEZ businesses tend to misuse them.

Some SEZ units show bogus profits from their operations since they do not have to pay any taxes on the same. It helps in increasing their creditworthiness in front of banks.

Some of the units that have operations outside the SEZ enclave, act as conduit to channelize profits from their other regions to their SEZ establishment in order to avoid levy of taxation outside.

One of the more prominent ways in which SEZ structure is misused for the purposes of Money Laundering is through software exports from Software Technology Parks (STPs). STPs are SEZ specifically designated for software companies.

This method also gains significance because of the fact that India has become a leading software exporter to the world earning huge amounts of foreign exchange for the country making this sector vulnerable to Money Laundering by some miscreants. Here is how.

The modus operandi:

Mr Darkhorse wants to bring some of his black money from overseas. He gets an export order from M/s Jockey & Co. of Dubai (his affiliate for Money Laundering purposes) to provide some software facilitating artificial intelligence in his company (a technically hi-fi order makes it easy to remit large sums of money).

Orders can be nothing more than simple e-mails containing few details of what is required and few jargons to make it appear genuine.

Then comes the delivery part which is funniest in case of exports of services and software. A few lines of programming can merit millions or nothing depending upon one's point of view. Therefore, it is very difficult to determine the value of a software. No tax or customs official is well equipped to determine the true worth of coding and that too when software imports and exports worth millions keep happening on daily basis.

Darkhorse receives payment from M/s Jockey & Co. which is nothing but his own income stashed in offshore shell corporations. Needless to say, Darkhorse can facilitate this transaction for many parties who want their money back from overseas. After procurement, the money will be transferred to them through contract of some goods or services.

Likewise, if Darkhorse wants to remit some illicit money overseas, either his own or that of his client, he would procure some software from Jockey and then remit the black money to him. Jockey will transfer this money to some offshore shell corporations controlled by Darkhorse.

Large amounts of black money get routed in this way over a period of time.

Under-Invoicing and Over-Invoicing methods, as discussed in the TBML chapter is exploited by money launderers using SEZ route.

POINTS TO PONDER:

Besides monetary benefits bestowed upon SEZ units, the following features further facilitate conversion of black money into white by them:

$ Many of the SEZ regulations are outdated.

$ SEZ units are able to deal with huge cash without any difficulty.

$ Compliance of Anti-Money Laundering regulations is not adequate.

$ Tax officials cannot search or invade a SEZ unit easily as it comes under supervision of a specifically designated SEZ administrative authority.

$ Many deductions with respect to expenses can be claimed by a SEZ unit just by self-certification.

$ In many Tax Haven countries, investors can buy companies off the shelf (Shelf Companies as discussed in the chapter on Offshore Shell Corporation) through a registered agent and by appointing a citizen of that country as partner/director. This requirement of a local partner is waived off in Free Trade Zones of many such countries.

METHOD 27

Gold, Diamonds, Gems and Jewellery: Let's Know a Bit More About Them

There is a lot of economics that keeps working behind gold, keeping economists and policy makers engaged in formulating various policies and strategies with respect to this glittering metal and its siblings. Siblings take the form of precious metal like platinum and gems like diamonds, sapphires, blue sapphires, emeralds, green emeralds, amber, topaz etc.

The metal 'Gold' has the potential to shake the whole economy of a country and significantly influence a country's trade surplus or deficit. Ironically however is the fact that this economic policy influencing metal has no economic use in itself.

It has only an *emotional value*, a shining metal whose shine and glitter is liked by human race since ages. Therefore, besides storing and investing in this metal, the only way it is put to use is by showing off, flaunting and attracting others. Since this metal is not available on the planet in abundance and its extraction from earth is difficult, the like of humans towards possessing this commodity goes crazy. Precious gems likewise are also scarcely available and need to be further cut and polished before they can attract the eyes of everyone.

Let us take a brief look on the characteristics of diamonds first before discussing how these precious gems are used for laundering money.

Characteristics of Diamonds:

1. **Diamonds as a currency and store of wealth:**

    The currency notes used in a country are mere paper or plastic with no inherent value. They are accepted as currency because of the promise made by governments to tender the amount written on them (which makes them a legal tender). Diamonds and other precious gems on the other hand do not carry any government's promise but have inherent value in them which makes them work as a parallel currency. The reasons for easy acceptance of diamonds as a parallel currency are manifold:

i. Diamonds are accepted globally. They have an international price set through international diamond bourses located across the world. They can be easily bought and sold outside the banking system.

ii. Diamonds have high Value to Mass Ratio i.e. Value ÷ Weight. It means the value stored in a small mass is very high which makes them an excellent store of wealth. Diamonds are weighed in carats where 1 carat = 0.20 grams = 200 mg = 0.00705 ounce and this small 200 mg piece with many others can easily fit in the pouch of anyone's wallet and then this small pouch will be worth tens of thousands of dollars, difficult to get detected.

iii. Diamonds have huge turnover in international trade.

iv. The Anti-Money Laundering Rules and Procedures which are applicable on a legal currency are not equally stringently applied over diamonds.

2. Valuation of Diamonds:

Valuation of diamonds is no joke. It takes real expertise in deciding upon the real value of a diamond.

In India, there is a proverb – *Ek here ke parakh ek jauhri hi kar sakta hai* meaning thereby that a diamond's real value is known only to an expert valuer in this field.

Diamonds are not just valued by weight. They are also valued on the basis of their individual count. Since they are small and precious stones, it is important to see how big an individual stone is and what is its weight.

For example: A one carat diamond can be a single stone weighing 1 carat (i.e. 200 mg or 0.2 grams) or it can be made up of around 100 micro diamonds, all weighing 0.1 carat on an average. The weight in both the cases is the same i.e. 1 carat but the value of 1 carat single diamond could be INR 500,000/- whereas that of 1 carat diamond made of multiple small ones could be INR 50,000/- only i.e. 10 times lesser than the individual stone.

Besides above, other features like shape and cut of a diamond – Round, Pear, Heart, Princess, Marquise, Oval and Cushion etc. can again change the value of a diamond considerably. For example a round shaped diamond has less value than a pear shaped one but it can change if round shaped is better cut than pear shaped. The cuts of diamond can vary from Fair Cut – Good – Very Good – Excellent – Ideal Cut. Then there are features like Colour, Clarity (Brightness) and even Depth Percentage among others that can change the value of a diamond.

As a thumb rule, there is 4Cs valuation methodology for valuing a diamond. The 4Cs are

1. The Carat Weight
2. The Crystalline Shape
3. The Colour and
4. The Clarity.

Experts therefore recommend that if one is buying diamond as an investment, he should value the Colour and Clarity on the top because when there is fluctuation in the market, these factors get highest weightage and become a benchmark for valuation whereas just valuing a stone on basis of weight is not commendable.

All this complexity in diamond valuation can lead to manipulation of its prices leading to emergence of black money and money laundering.

3. **Stark difference between value of Rough Diamond and Cut Diamond:**

Diamonds when extracted from earth either from rocks or waterbeds are completely different from what we are used to seeing them as a glittering stone. Diamonds are produced either by mining hard rocks known as *kimberlitic* rocks or by extracting them from *alluvial* deposits across river beds, sea floor or sea beds.

The value of a rough diamond is far less than that of a polished one. Depending upon the aforementioned 4C factors, value of a rough diamond can increase from a few thousand INR ('000s) to Tens of Millions of INRs ('0,000,000s) on its cutting and polishing.

4. **International connectivity and trade in Diamonds:**

$ Russia, Australia, Canada and South, Central and West African countries are rich in rough diamond reserves.

$ Bulk of cutting and polishing of rough diamonds takes place in India, Israel, Belgium and China.

$ Diamond trading (through bourses) is more prominent in UK, U.A.E and U.S.

This shows how the world is inter-connected and how easy it is to settle dues in diamonds across the world. As an Indian, I am proud of the fact that most of the cutting and polishing of diamonds is done in India today but we also need to think; Doesn't that makes India more vulnerable to Money Laundering activities arising out of diamond trade.

5. **Kimberley Certification and the loopholes therein:**

As stated above, Kimberley is the rock from where diamonds are extracted and so the name Kimberley Certification. The 'Kimberley Process Certification Scheme (KPCS)' is briefly explained as follows:

In 1970s and thereafter till the formulation of KPCS in 2003, there were many diamond rich countries like Angola, Ivory Coast, Congo, Liberia etc. (all in Africa) where governments were not stable and civil unrest was quite common. The anti-government organisations in these countries used to fund their fight against their respective governments through diamond exports. They used to illegally extract the diamonds (such diamonds are known as conflict diamonds or blood diamonds) in these countries and then sell these diamonds to fight with government. To curb the finances of these anti-government forces, United Nations came out with a certification process known as KPCS. Some of the primary objectives and salient features of KPCS are as follows:

1. The participating countries need to ensure that diamonds originating from their territories are not financing the rebels i.e. they are not conflict / blood diamonds.

2. No diamond can be exported to or imported from a non-participating country.

3. The revenues from the diamond export will be used in government approved schemes and objectives.

4. Diamonds by participating countries will not be bought from suspect sources or unknown suppliers even if they are from participating countries.

5. Every Diamond Import/Export will be accompanied by a certificate known as **Kimberley Certificate** which certifies that the source is legitimate. This certificate is issued by the export promotion body of the exporting country and thus the origin and source are well documented. If the rough diamonds imported by a country are being re-exported, then such country will issue a fresh Kimberley Certificate.

There is no doubt that KPCS with more than 80 participating countries (African and Non-African exporters) in the world has largely been able to achieve its main objective of curbing financing for civil unrest to a large extent but its role in curbing Money Laundering is doubted by many.

The reason is **'Commingling'**. Commingling here means mixing the illicit diamonds (a form of black money) with legitimate ones and it gains significance in the context of Money Laundering with respect to Diamonds Trade.

We know Money Laundering is all about conversion of illicit money (Dirty Money or Black Money) into legitimate money (Clean Money or White Money). So mixing of the Dirty Money – in form of diamonds with white money – legitimate diamonds is nothing but facilitation of Money Laundering.

The loopholes that help this to happen are:

1. Kimberley Process Certification is not applicable to cut and polished diamonds. It is only applicable to rough diamonds.

2. Kimberley Process Certification is not applicable if rough diamonds are sold/ traded locally within a country.

Thus anyone possessing illegally earned rough diamonds can cut and polish them locally and then trade them internationally without the need to furnish a Kimberley Certificate (KC). Similarly the cut and polished diamonds obtained from legitimate rough diamonds coming under KC are mixed (commingled) with other similarly cut and polished diamonds obtained illegally. This comingling converts the illicit diamonds into a parallel currency and also keeps its source under wraps.

It is noteworthy to point that the size and shape of a diamond can be changed completely by cutting and re-cutting it. This makes it more complicated and difficult for the investigative authorities to trace it back to its original illicit form of rough diamond. There can be one and many diamonds that can be cut from a rough diamond and absence of stringent rules worldwide to document the origin of diamonds in case of trading of cut and polished diamonds means that there is no significant audit trail left.

Since the value of a diamond gets unlocked from few thousands to few millions only after it is cut and polished, the absence of a Kimberley kind of process in trading of polished diamonds makes it a perfect Money Laundering scheme.

The result of all of the above features combined is that diamonds are easily used in Money Laundering activities. Its characteristic of wide acceptability nationally and internationally and ability to cross international borders with ease undoubtedly makes it a currency of choice for money launderers.

Coming to modus operandi in Money Laundering through diamonds:

Modus Operandi 1: Commingling

As explained above, the illicit diamonds are mixed with legitimate diamonds and the pool becomes one. It is also difficult to track an illicit rough diamond once it has been cut and polished. The payment for the illicit diamond is made in black whereas the payment for the legitimate one comes in white.

Modus Operandi 2: Use of Diamonds as a store of wealth and as a currency

Black Money holders use diamonds to store their black money due to its high value to mass ratio. Further it can be easily transported from one place to another and is globally acceptable.

Modus Operandi 3: TBML in Diamonds

As discussed, it is difficult to value a diamond. The principle of 4Cs applies here of which the 'Carat' weight is just one. Other Cs which affect the valuation significantly are the cut or the shape better known as the 'Crystalline' shape, the 'Colour' and the 'Clarity'. So unless one is expert in measuring all the 4Cs and everything else required to value a diamond, room for manipulation always remains. The problem gets amplified with the absence of a price list for diamonds.

Thus, if a person wants to stash his black money overseas, he will approach a diamond exporter who would under-invoice his export consignment by the required amount and when the black money holder wants his black money back from overseas, the exporter will over invoice his export consignment. *We have seen these schemes in our TBML chapter.*

Since diamond trade is a high value game involving millions and billions of rupees, laundering high amounts is easy by over pricing or under-pricing the consignment in the range of 5–15%. Customs officers are not experts in valuation of diamonds and even if they engage the services of a technical valuer, it is not plausible to check each and every piece of diamond that is exported or imported.

Furthermore, the ease of doing business requirements have compelled many governments to rely on self-assessed valuations. In many countries it is not even mandatory to value diamonds accurately considering all 4Cs and valuation only based upon carat weight is deemed satisfactory.

Modus Operandi 4: Manipulation of Inventory Records:

The closing inventory plays an important role in determining the profit from a business and hence Income Tax payable on it. If the closing inventory is shown at a value lower than true value, profit will be lesser and therefore Income Tax applicable there upon. Thus, if a business house manipulates the true value of a diamond and records it only by weight instead of taking other factors into account, it will show drastically reduced profit and hence low tax payable, taking advantage of complexity of diamond valuation.

Since closing stock of one year becomes opening stock of another year, the benefit of showing lower inventory value at the yearend will extinguish next year. Therefore business houses will keep on manipulating the inventory figures year on year, giving them the advantage of lower tax payable every year. This coupled with increase in business volumes becomes an icing on the cake for them as then the manipulation of inventory becomes even less visible. Manipulation of closing stock is used not just in diamonds but other businesses as well to evade taxes.

Like diamonds, there exists room for manipulation of other precious metals and stones like Gold, Platinum, Emerald and Sapphire etc.

All these precious metals and stones are easy store of wealth and are acceptable globally.

Moreover, price of gold is determined internationally and has low fluctuation relative to stocks and other commodities. Because of its international price fixation, international listing and trading, global acceptability, high liquidity and low volatility, it is also considered as a safe investment and hedge against inflation. All this makes it lucrative for black money holders and money launderers.

Many jewellers do not keep proper inventory records of these precious metals and stones leading to a whole black money economy. They sell their unaccounted inventory and accept black money. This black money is used to purchase more inventories in unaccounted form that ultimately leads to unaccounted imports of these goods (i.e. smuggling).

Sometimes even data on export of gold by one country to India and import of gold in India from that country does not match. This difference is only a part of smuggling. It may even happen that some consignments are not recorded by both (exporting and importing) the countries. Smuggling increases when government levies taxes on trading of these precious items.

Please note that buying gold or other precious gems and jewellery although helps in stashing of black money but such gems and jewellery bought remains black only. Thus there is no money laundering aspect as such which refers to conversion of black money into white.

POINTS TO PONDER:

$ With the advent of technology, now cut and polished diamonds are also being marked for various identifications which have made its valuation relatively easy and going forward, it will also enable differentiation between polished diamonds coming out of legitimate and illegitimate rough diamonds.

$ In India, government knows the issues well and is committed to eradication of black money. It is taking various measures to bring in transparency in trading of gold and diamonds.

METHOD 28

Bitcoins and Digital Currencies: Understanding their 'Wow' Effect

D igital currency also known as crypto currency is the opposite of fiat money. Fiat money is the currency which the government of a country has declared as its legal tender. In plain terms, it is the currency of our daily use. So, being opposite; Digital Currency has no legal backing from any government and is not a currency of daily use. However, such is the power of the digital currency that it is being seen as a competitor of fiat currency and governments across the globe, impressed by the system are looking to develop digital currencies of their own.

Digital currency in current times is technologically the most advanced method used for hiding and laundering black money.

There have been various digital currencies used actively over the past few years and have since evolved. 'Bitcoin' at present is the most prominent form of digital money. It has many takers across the world who happily sell their goods and services for bitcoins in return.

For understanding purposes, this chapter is broadly divided into two parts. The first part explains what a bitcoin is and how it functions, the second part tells why bitcoins are lucrative for illicit money transfers and how they are used for this purpose.

Part 1: Bitcoin - An infamous digital currency

Please note that bitcoins stored in a bitcoin wallet is not the same as money stored in an electronic wallet. The e-wallets carry fiat currency and not digital currency.

However, if I have got some bitcoins in my bitcoin wallet from where I want to buy something and the seller is ready to accept these bitcoins, then the transaction becomes as simple as transfer of money from any e-wallet like PayPal or Paytm.

Bitcoin is a digital currency and a digital currency is not a Real, Tangible or Official Currency. It means you can never touch a bitcoin and no government on this planet (or corporation for that matter) promises to pay even a single penny for this currency.

But still if it is not a real currency, it is not unreal too. It commands value through trading and is accepted by sellers and merchants across the globe. As of now (Dec' 2016) 1 Bitcoin comes for USD 750 (equivalent to INR 51,000/-) and its value has increased from USD 400 as of Dec' 2015. As of Feb' 2017, its value is hovering around USD 1000 (equivalent to INR 68,000).

The world of Bitcoin: Simplified

$ 'Bitcoin' when written with B in capital letter refers to Bitcoin network, systems and its users as a whole and 'bitcoin' with b in small refers to the digital currency. *(I may not have followed this protocol very strictly)*

$ Bitcoin or any digital currency for the matter is just an algorithm. Only a piece of programming, nothing else. (But a very complex piece of programming indeed)

$ Bitcoin programme was originally designed by Mr Satoshi Nakamoto (pseudonymous name of the originator) and released in 2009. Since then software experts from across the globe have been improving, evolving, debugging (removing errors) and perfecting this system. The system has been designed in such a way that if it gets benefited or strengthened by anyone, that technician is rewarded with free bitcoins by the system itself.

$ Bitcoin is a beautiful system where there is no authority that regulates, manages or keeps its records. The problem of nobody managing its accounts and records gets resolved by giving the accounting book (ledger) to everyone using this system. Anybody who cares to look can verify the records. That's why it's called distributed ledger.

$ Whenever a Bitcoin transaction takes place, it automatically gets recorded in the said everybody's ledger – Public Database. This ledger contains details of every single bitcoin transaction that ever happened in the past or is happening in the present.

$ The concept of shared accounting book –is technically known as Blockchain Technology (here, the transaction data is recorded in files called blocks and these blocks are organised in a linear sequence). This database is severely encrypted and hence the name crypto currency given to Bitcoin and other similar digital currencies.

$ Bitcoin is an encrypted system where all transfer of funds is coded so that no person other than the one intended to be able to view or intercept. This coding happens through the use of 'Public Key and Private Key' also known as 'Encryption key and Decryption key' as shown in the diagram below:

$ To send and receive bitcoins, one needs to download a Bitcoin Wallet as the first and foremost step. Bitcoin Wallet is an application just like any other mobile app. It contains both a public key as well as a private key and is used to receive, store and transfer bitcoins. An example is 'Coinbase' which is a widely used Bitcoin Wallet in more than

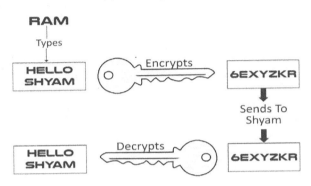

30 countries. In India some common Bitcoin wallets are BTXIndia and Unocoin.

$ Any person can get bitcoins for use either by buying bitcoins from an online bitcoin exchange, selling some goods or services for bitcoins or by approving bitcoin transactions by solving some mathematical puzzles (commonly known as bitcoin mining and explained a bit later). Bitcoins are also earned as reward by strengthening the Bitcoin system.

$ Once there, bitcoins can be transferred to any other person in this world using the recipient's bitcoin address which is like his account number on this network.

$ Bitcoin Address is the address of a Bitcoin user's wallet. It can be linked to be something like our e-mail address which is made available to everyone publicly. Anyone who wants to send me an e-mail will use my e-mail address and I will then view it by entering the pass code of my e-mail address. Similarly a person who wants to send me some bitcoins will use my Bitcoin Address.

Technically, this address is a pairing of a hashed (shortened) public key and a private key.

Example of Private Key: 5K3EwLxyzabcQebkS4TEVC1mxNFcz4rk72C4rkV6thZoPi

Example of Hashed (shortened) Public Key: 16mvf3wy9kzCotN9aDHofS8q

Example of Bitcoin Address: 1BvBMSEYstQetqFn5au

$ When a bitcoin (1 BTC) is transferred from Mr X to Mr Y, this transaction is first recorded in a public ledger (Blockchain) and from there it is picked by Bitcoin users across the globe who will verify the ownership of Mr X by checking the past transactions of the bitcoin in question and once satisfied will approve the transaction from X to Y. These people are called miners and they charge transaction fees (a small percentage of the whole transaction) for approving this transaction.

$ These miners not only approve the bitcoin transaction for fees but also bring new bitcoins into circulation by earning rewards for approving the transactions. Mining is the process of printing bitcoins in layman terms. In case of real currencies, the central banks in consultations with governments decide how much additional currency needs to be printed. But since there is no regulator for Bitcoin, the protocols embedded in the programming itself decides how much more bitcoins are needed to be in circulation while benefitting the whole system at the same time.

$ Miners get new bitcoins as reward for approving the transactions. The reward being given by the system to miners is reducing gradually. By design, it gets halved after every 4 years. At inception, it was 50 BTC for each block and now it has reduced to 25 BTC per block and since it takes ~ 10 minutes for a block to get confirmed, it means 25 new bitcoins come into existence (get mined) every 10 minutes. Although the number of new bitcoins per block will reduce gradually over period of time but it will be compensated by higher transaction fees in future. It is stated that the Bitcoin system is so designed that ~95% of bitcoins will come into existence in next 10 years, ~99% will exist by the year 2033 and the last BTC will come out in the year 2140.

$ A miner's chance of verifying a transaction depends upon his system's computational power compared with that of other miners working on that transaction. As more and more miners are entering the system, the difficulty level is increasing by every passing day. In this system, a miner or group of them working collectively must control at least 51% of computational power available in the network at that point of time so that the remaining 49% miners are not able to allow double spending of a transaction.

$ Easier said than done. The mining mentioned above is not simple by any means. The verification of a transaction by checking all the past transactions has a difficulty factor embedded into it which is required to be solved to complete the block chain accurately. It needs super-duper computational power for which specialised hardware (manufactured by Bitcoin specialist companies) having high speed computational efficiency is used by miners.

$ The concept of mining and Blockchain technology revolves around a predominant question -what if I have a bitcoin and I transfer it to 2 or more persons.

$ We know that every user who is present on Bitcoin network has downloaded a wallet which is connected to the database and therefore when I transfer 1 BTC to say 2 people – Mr X and Mr Y simultaneously say from different devices, it is a problem. This problem has even got a technical name - double spending. One of this transaction will not be complete but only if it is not approved by Bitcoin system.

$ When I do a transaction, my wallet (client in jargon) broadcasts this signal to the entire network. (It will first broadcast this signal to the nodes (computers/ clients/ users) to which it is connected, say 10. Then each of these 10 nodes send this transaction signal to the other nodes to which they are connected and likewise the message spreads over the network, that's why it is called Peer to Peer (P2P) network).

$ After that, experts from across the globe pick this transaction for verification/ background check. They brainstorm with their high end processing machines to find out whether the proposed transaction is authentic in every aspect i.e. whether I am valid owner of the BTC or not, whether the person from whom I got the bitcoin was also a valid owner of that BTC or not and so on.

$ After verifying the past transactions, they establish my right to transfer this BTC other person. If the majority of miners solve this block and approve this transaction, the transaction is allowed but it is still not added to the Blockchain and remains reversible. It is finally confirmed and approved of as irreversible by the system only after 5 more blocks of transactions have been added and confirmed after which it is assumed that transaction was authentic and becomes irreversible.

$ This means Blockchain technology ensures safety and security of the transactions through a system where users themselves vouch for authenticity of the transactions and get paid in return. Currently, it takes around ~10 minutes of time for 1 block of transactions to get added to the chain so it will take around ~60 minutes for a transaction to get confirmed and become irreversible (10 minutes for the transaction block and 10 minutes each for the next five blocks). This is sufficient time for the miners across the world to check that no problem has occurred from a particular transaction which was done 60 minutes before and all the blocks of data are getting solved in time.

$ In my case, since I transferred my BTC to Mr X as well as to Mr Y at the same time, chances are that 50% of the miners will approve the transfer to X and

50% will approve it to Y and so the transaction will not take place and if it so happens that 51% or more approve it for X (or may be Y); In that case, it will get transferred to X (or Y as the case may be) and to no other person and after 5 more blocks of transactions are added, this transaction becomes irreversible. Thus no double spending of same BTC.

$ Miners work individually as well as collectively in a group and share the rewards and transaction fees between themselves. In this way, Bitcoin is a full banking system in itself which keeps getting improved and perfected regularly.

$ Since miners are rewarded in form of bitcoins (either new or existing through transaction fees) whose value will increase only with the increase in value of Bitcoin system, they have a vested interest in perfecting the functioning of this system.

$ Now coming to the price of bitcoin. As per the design of the programme, there can be a maximum of 21 Million Bitcoins that can come into existence and not even a single more will ever exist. At present, there are around 16.2 Million Bitcoins in circulation. So where is the remaining? Nowhere. They are yet to be brought or extracted into existence through the mining process. They are getting mined at a constant rate. ~95% will come into existence by 2026, 99% by 2033 and last one in 2041. The supply of bitcoins is thus limited and this is where the value of bitcoins is derived.

$ Here, one may be curious to know as to what will happen after all 21 Million Bitcoins have been mined and start circulating. Will it put an end to this network or be disadvantageous for it?

$ Having a limited number of 21 Million bitcoins is another unique feature of Bitcoin and this is in no way a limitation of the system because transactions in bitcoins can be denominated in smaller sub-units of a bitcoin. 1 bitcoin is equal to 100 Million (10^8) individual units called bits and therefore a bitcoin is divisible up to 8 decimals depending upon the transaction size. So don't worry if you need to buy a chocolate or a cup of coffee with bitcoin, it is easily divisible into smaller parts.

$ The price of bitcoin is determined in the same way as that of any other commodity in the world i.e. based upon the last transaction (traded) price and forces of demand and supply playing in the hindsight. It is an astonishing fact that that in 2010, when the currency was not even a year old, its value was in few cents. Gossips make rounds that 1 BTC was equal to 2 Pizzas at that time and this value of 1 BTC rose to USD 32 in 2011, USD 1200 in 2013, went down to USD 600 in 2014, USD 250 in 2015 and hovers around USD 750 at present. Tremendous volatility shows tremendous fluctuating interest in this currency.

$ Since the supply is limited, if the demand increases, the price of bitcoin is bound to go up. The value of 1 Bitcoin currently is around USD 1,000 which gives a cue about the total amount of bitcoins in circulation, 16.2 Mio bitcoins x USD 1,000 = USD 16.2 Billion of market capitalisation which is quite small compared to the GDP (Gross Domestic Product) of USA at ~USD 10 trillion and miniscule in front of world GDP at more USD 42 Trillion. Thus the amount is not big at all considering it is the biggest opponent of fiat currency as of date and USD 16.2 Billion is only a fraction of all fiat currency circulating in this world.

A Bitcoin payment transaction is as simple as: A user transferring 1 BTC from his bitcoin Wallet to another person's bitcoin Wallet.	Technically it can be as complicated as follows: A user generates a request to send one bitcoin from his account using a mobile or computer. The request floats on Bitcoin network till it picked up by miners for processing. During mining, transactions are packed into data blocks and are assigned a random header. Miners compete with each other to match the block's header with a nonce (an arbitrary number used only once in a cryptographic communication) to generate a short alphanumeric code called hash. If this hash is accepted by the Bitcoin network, the transaction is approved and carried out and the hash generator gets bitcoins in rewards. These hash values are then added to the next block's header creating a block chain which serves as a database or public ledger of all bitcoin transactions made till date.

Bitcoin Mining

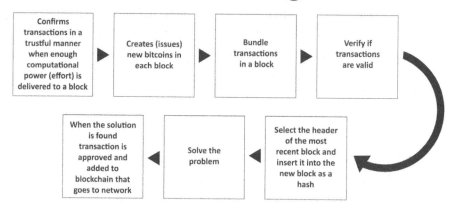

Part 2: Bitcoin - Lucrative for illicit payments

If you found part 1 complex and difficult to understand, you have understood one feature of Bitcoin that makes it lucrative for stashing of wealth and making illicit payments. Some other features are as follows:

- ✓ There is no regulator of Bitcoin and no requirement of any Bank or Financial Institution to do a transaction on Bitcoin network.

- ✓ In Bitcoin system, a person can create as many Bitcoin addresses as he desires without disclosing an iota of his true identity. Moreover, there can be different addresses created for undertaking different transactions.

- ✓ Bitcoin enjoys its reputation as an anonymous currency but in reality it is a pseudonymous one since all the public addresses (despite of their fictitious ID) are linked to the IP address (Unique code) of user's device. However, launderers use anonymity providing software and browsers such as The Onion Router (TOR) and 'Darkwallet' specially coded for Bitcoin network which can hide a user's IP Address or broadcast incorrect information about the same.

- ✓ Darkwallet uses a technique which integrates anonymity into all transactions of its users. Every time a user spends bitcoins, his transaction is combined with any transaction of another user being made at the same time. For example If Darkhorse is buying drugs from a prohibited site and Whitehorse is buying a toy from an online toy store, Darkwallet will combine these two transactions and encrypt them into in to a single movement of funds after which no investigator is able to easily determine whose coins went where.

- ✓ Many tax havens are contemplating to promote and increase the use of Bitcoin without any restriction from their land.

- ✓ In India, KYC documents are needed only to buy or sell bitcoins but a user can receive and send bitcoins, buy and sell goods through bitcoins without completing any verification.

- ✓ There are minimal regulations and awareness as to the use of Bitcoins which results in bleak chances of catching the black money stashed in Bitcoin network. Bitcoin holdings are rarely revealed accurately to the tax authorities as they are not well equipped to find them on their own.

- ✓ There remains ambiguity in taxation with respect to bitcoins. It is not clear if bitcoin is a currency, commodity or a security like equity or bond. No such clarity leads to no Capital Gains tax if the value of bitcoins appreciated before sale. For example: X bought 500 BTC at USD 350 and sold them at USD 750 within a year. There is no clarity if this Capital Gains is taxable or not. Then, non-disclosure of bitcoin holdings lead to further evasion of tax.

All this makes it easy for black money holders to launder their ill-gotten gains through Bitcoin:

Modus Operandi 1:

Mr Darkhorse has INR 10 Million of black money.

Step 1: Darkhorse downloads a Bitcoin Wallet on his smart phone.

Step 2: He creates a Bitcoin Account.

Step 3: He approaches Mr Jockey who is a black racketeering agent in Bitcoin and hands over his black money to him.

Step 4: Jockey transfers equivalent amount of Bitcoins (excluding his commission) to the Bitcoin Address of Darkhorse.

Money hidden/ money laundered.

In a similar way, Darkhorse can stash his black money in Bitcoins instead of remitting it to any offshore shell corporation. A famous newspaper recently reported that bitcoins have the potential to make offshore tax havens empty.

Why money hidden becomes money laundered?

- ✓ Once the money gets converted into bitcoins, it gets hidden as it gets converted into some alphanumeric strings called the Bitcoin Address and the private key. No one knows that Mr Darkhorse has got a Bitcoin Account as his asset. He will definitely not have this account in his real name and neither will he have only a single bitcoin account.

✓ The only space required to possess this asset is 1 inch of paper that has the private key of the account written over it. This account can be accessed and used by Darkhorse from any corner of the world. Thus his invisible money keeps travelling with him and is always available for spending as well as conversion into cash. Darkhorse has 1 BTC of Black Money. Current Exchange Rate is say 1 BTC = USD 750. Darkhorse transfers 1 BTC to Jockey and receives USD 740 in cash. Money Laundered

✓ Then, there are numerous companies across the globe selling through bitcoin every item that is worth selling on internet. All big companies across industries accept Bitcoins. Many big consultancy companies and even universities accept bitcoins too and the number is increasing every day.

✓ One reason for such an increase in acceptance of bitcoins is Tax Evasion. If you sell through bitcoins, the sale is hidden and thus there is no incidence of taxation. No one knows how much sales have you done through bitcoins and through which addresses. It's all anonymous.

✓ Moving a step further, don't be surprised if I tell you that there are more than 400 ATM machines which can dispense cash for equivalent of Bitcoins.

✓ These Bitcoin ATMs spread across the globe (not in India as of now) do not dispense bitcoins but a person can deposit his cash in the machine and his Bitcoin Wallet will get credited with equivalent bitcoins. Similarly, in case he has got bitcoins in his wallet, he can collect equivalent cash from these machines.

✓ Mr Darkhorse can deposit his black money directly in his Bitcoin Account through these ATMs. Since these ATMs are in developed countries, he will be taking care of breaking the amount in multiple transactions (below USD 10,000/- threshold applicable on a single cash transaction in United States).

✓ It will be noteworthy to point that Bitcoin although the most popular digital / crypto currency in use in the current times is just one of its kinds. Litecoin, Peercoin, Gridcoin, Mastercoin, Monero are some of the alternatives with distinguished and more secure features waiting for their turn to rise to the ranks of Bitcoin. A professional money launderer fully aware of the benefits of diversification will not put all his eggs in one basket would definitely be using all of these and many more complicated schemes to launder his Dirty Money.

Modus Operandi 2:

Darkhorse has USD 1 Million of black money which he wants to convert into white.

Step 1: Darkhorse downloads a Bitcoin Wallet on his smart phone.

Step 2: He creates a Bitcoin Account.

Step 3: Darkhorse approaches M/s Jockey and cartel – A Bitcoin Mining group headed by Jockey. Darkhorse hands over his black money of USD 1 Million to Jockey for laundering. The money is smurfed into banking accounts of the cartel and equivalent amount of bitcoins purchased are credited in their wallets.

Step 4: M/s Jockey and his cartel continue their mining (verification) transactions for earning transaction fees as well as reward Bitcoins from the system but with a small difference - *They are now verifying the transactions in the name of Mr Darkhorse so that the income is credited to his account.*

Step 5: Jockey does many frivolous activities to increase the income of Darkhorse. He asks his cartel to approve various frivolous / orchestrated circular transactions over the network with an objective of earning heavy transaction fees. The cartel circulates their own bitcoins amongst themselves in a cautious manner so that miners from outside the group don't get to approve these transactions prior to them. Since the parties to the transaction and the transaction approvers know each other's movements in advance and can even perform all these roles interchangeably, outsiders don't stand a fair chance and keep out.

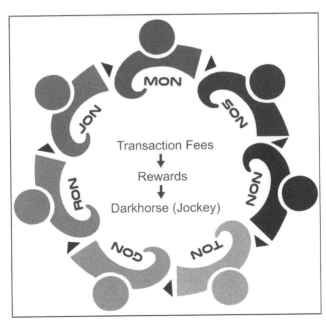

The cartel members and their affiliates do circular transactions between them and on each transaction pay hefty fees to Jockey and his group acting through the mining account in the name of Darkhorse. For example: Mon transfers USD 1 Million of BTC to Son and pays transaction fees @2% i.e. USD 20,000 to Jockey (Darkhorse) for approval of this transaction. The amount of such a transaction and the transaction fees can be increased by them as and when they want. Technically, they can route any amount of money between themselves any number of times without any restriction because it's all circular between them.

Once they have collected the requite amount of USD 1 Million in form of transaction fees and reward points in BTC in Darkhorse's account over a period of time; Darkhorse wire transfers the money into his legal account. Money Laundered.

By the way, Darkhorse did learn some Bitcoin jargon to show off in front of investigators that he actually did BTC mining.

POINTS TO PONDER:

$ The biggest risk Bitcoin faces is that of loss by hacking. If you hold hundreds and thousands of Bitcoins in your bitcoin wallet and they are stolen in an attack by hackers, what will you do? Cyber Crime Cell of Police will be hardly of any help. These coins have no backing by any government so you cannot go any Bank or monetary authority claiming compensation for laxity in security features. And it will be more of your undisclosed money, right?

$ News of Bitcoins getting hacked is a plenty. They are hacked by the technicians who deal with it in and out. Hacking is also a reason for sharp volatility in the price of Bitcoins. Whenever, there is any news of hacking, the price goes down and when the system gets strengthened against it, the price goes up.

$ 51% Attack: There looms a risk of 51% attack on Bitcoin. If majority of the computational power can be controlled by someone then he can do anything on the system. Although the Bitcoin system is getting bigger and stronger by every passing day and is beyond the control of any single person, group or geography but if the governments of few powerful countries decide, they can cause this system go hay wire by investing and millions and billions of dollars in a bid to control majority of the computational power.

$ 'Silkroad' was an online black market in USA which sold illegal drugs in exchange for Bitcoins. It was shut down by FBI (Federal Bureau of Investigation) in 2013 and its promoter Mr Ross William Ulbricht also got arrested despite the fact that website used TOR software to maintain anonymity.

$ There are news reports that Satoshi Nakamoto's true identity has been revealed. Recently, an Australian Entrepreneur – Craig Steven Wright identified himself as the creator of Bitcoin under the pseudonym Satoshi Nakamoto but is disputed by many prominent members of Bitcoin community and this is not for the first time, someone has claimed himself to be Satoshi Nakamoto.

METHOD 28

Gambling

E arning money by illegitimate ways and then laundering it while betting at casinos and exotic racing clubs. How Envious!!

If you win in gambling, you get a receipt and then the jackpot amount is wire transferred to your legal bank account. This all legal proposition makes gambling a big bet for money launderers. So, when hooked by investigators to explain source of huge amounts of money, Mr Darkhorse has to just say that he is a gambler and then prove it by showing the winning receipt. Sounds great! Let us see how the plan is executed.

Since a bettor cannot be booked for losing money over betting, he similarly cannot be booked for winning money from such betting. So, unless there are clear regulations over gambling, all that a winning money launderer has to do is pay taxes on his winnings to the government. It is amazing that certain jurisdictions impose nil or minimal tax on gambling jackpots.

Please note that since India has restrictions on gambling, the methods stated here are more common overseas.

Modus Operandi 1: The crude way of doing it

Darkhorse has INR 1 Million of black money which he wants to launder into white. He finds Mr Jockey who is a casino operator and ready to do anything for his casino's business.

Darkhorse hands over his INR 1 Million to Jockey who in return hands over 4 to 5 winning receipts to Darkhorse totalling INR 0.85 Million keeping INR 0.15 Mio as his gaming fees and commission. These winning receipts may be of a single day or staggered over a period of few months.

Mr Jockey would have documented everything in order. Hundreds of people would have played in his casino during the aforementioned period totalling that extra INR 1 Million of which Darkhorse is a registered winner. Jockey then transfers this amount to Darkhorse's account and Darkhorse pays appropriate tax on winnings. Money Laundered.

Please note that:

✓ Darkhorse would have actually visited this casino during the aforesaid period and played like a professional gambler at least for the CCTV (Closed Circuit Television) footage.

✓ CCTV Cameras may not always be compulsory and working in order to show all games in detail.

✓ AML systems are well in place in Jockey's casino but sometimes they work more on his instructions than they are required legally.

✓ This scheme can be used by Darkhorse in casinos, horse racing clubs or any other games/sports where betting is permitted.

Modus Operandi 2: The sophisticated way of doing it

This modus operandi works on the concept of 'Fixed Odds' in betting.

Fixed Odds Betting (FOB) means that the bettor is aware of the amount he stands to win and lose at the time of placing the bet with fixed probabilities attached to these amounts.

Example: A player bets INR 100 on a market at odds of 1/1 and a bookmaker (betting company) accepts this bet. It implies that the player and book maker stake equal amount (1:1). They will either lose full or win double their bet amount.

In this type of gambling, a person can continue playing the gamble by placing bets on the contrasting mutually exclusive outcomes without losing a single penny. (Of course, he will pay the gaming fee which is never much to deter the money launderers).

Fixed Odds can be played in many games. Let us look at it via game of roulette.

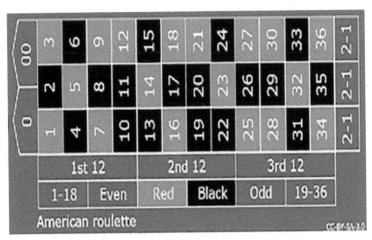

181

Roulette is one of the prominent games played in any casino worldwide.

Players, usually up to eight, play against the House represented by the croupier also called the dealer, who spins the roulette wheel and handles the wagers and payouts.

In the European roulette version, the wheel has 37 slots representing 36 numbers and 1 zero. In the USA most roulette wheels have 2 zeros and therefore 38 slots.

Each player buys-in a different coloured chips so their bets don't get mixed up. At the end of play, if you won, you exchange back the coloured chips with cash chips. Cash chips are special chips with their exchange value amount imprinted on them. There are several denominations in various colours. These chips can be exchanged at the cash desk for the actual amount of cash.

To play roulette, one places a bet or bets on numbers (any number including the zero) in the table layout or on the outside, and when everybody at the table had a chance to place their bets, the croupier starts the spin and launches the ball.

Just a few moments before the ball is about to drop over the slots, the croupier says 'no more bets'. From that moment no one is allowed to place - or change - their bets until the ball drops on a slot. Only after the croupier places the dolly on the winning number on the roulette table and clears all the losing bets, one can start placing his new bets while the croupier pays the winner. The winners are those bets that are on or around the number that comes up. Also the bets on the outside of the layout win if the winning number is represented.

There is a house advantage (or fees of the casinos) which is deducted from the winner's money. It is around ~3% on a single zero roulette table and ~8% on a double zero roulette table.

Since there are numbers ranging 1 to 36 as well as a '0' and in some cases '00' too. Thus, one can bet on these 38 numbers either singularly or with some combinations.

He can conversely also bet on combinations like all Red, all Black, all Even, all Odd, any of 1st 12 (1 to 12), any of 2nd 12 (13 to 24), any of 3rd 12 (25 to 36).

In case, he places bets on 'Red', his money gets doubled if the ball lands on 'Red' and he loses full if the ball lands on 'black'. Similarly, his money gets tripled in case he bets on '2nd 12' and the ball lands on 13 but he loses full money if ball lands on any number other than 13 to 24.

Launderer's strategy:

A money launderer's strategy is therefore quite simple and common: INR 20 on black, INR 20 on red and INR 2 on zero. A press of the button and the wheel spins; if the ball lands on red or black, he loses full on one bet and doubles his money on the other. So it's a loss of INR 2 (and the house advantage fees). The money placed on the zero (INR 2/-) is the only risk he is taking with his money. If the ball does land on zero, he wins INR 72.

He forgets the money lost, en-cashes his chips and takes the winning receipt for the amount won.

Money laundered.

Similarly, he could have placed bets on all three - 1st 12, 2nd 12 and 3rd 12. He would lose equal money on two and treble his money on third. Money Laundered.

The concept is simple that the bettor takes advantage of fixed probabilities associated with the outcomes by making contrasting bets.

To obfuscate the CCTV footage and player records, Darkhorse plays these games with professional gamblers who team up with him at game tables in such a manner that no one understands who is actually winning and who is losing between them. Darkhorse, however always emerges as the declared winner.

Many jurisdictions are facilitators of Money Laundering by promoting gambling. They promote gambling to earn heavy revenues from the industry through taxes and license fees, benefit from tourism and promote employment generation through their many verticals like bars, restaurants, hotels, tour operations etc.

Macau is the new Mecca of gambling after Las Vegas. In India too, we have many casinos in Goa. Now days, with the advent of technology and globalisation; Mr Darkhorse can win in a casino located in say Singapore and take winning proceeds in any other jurisdiction of his choice say Las Vegas. Then there are Hawala operators too who facilitate this game; Mr Darkhorse can go to Dubai without carrying any money, take money from Mr Jockey who is a Hawala operator there, play in casinos of Dubai, win/lose whatever, shop in the shopping festival and then travel back to his home country. Money will be collected by Jockey's men from his doorstep.

Why forget the use of Bitcoins and TBML through which Darkhorse has stashed millions of his black money overseas. That money is easily available at his disposal for gambling.

Modus Operandi 3: Online Gambling

Games like roulette, poker and bingo etc. are very popular on the internet. Their popularity spares no money launderer from trying his hands on them.

There are hundreds of international jurisdictions that regulate thousands of internet gambling websites - the licensed ones and for every one licensed website, there are at least 10 un-licensed websites running.

The key difference between licensed and un-licensed gambling websites is that the licensed ones adhere to AML procedures; they are audited by the supervisory authorities whereas un-licensed ones are just fly by night operators.

The payment processing in online gaming takes place when a player deposits or withdraws money from an operator. The player chooses a deposit option, for example a credit card, a debit card, a prepaid card, online banking, demand draft, traveller's cheque etc. If say the payment is made by credit card, the payment processor will transfer the funds from his credit card to an account of the gambling operator who then credits the balance to the player's account.

Similarly, after playing the game, the player can opt for a payment option to withdraw his money. He can get it credited to his debit card or credit card or can wire transfer the money to his bank account.

The value chain for deposits and withdrawals is depicted as follows:

Value Chain of Deposits:

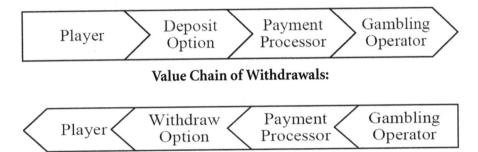

Value Chain of Withdrawals:

Example:

Mr Darkhorse has INR 1 Million of black money which he wants to launder into white.

He opens an account with one of the online casino operators, verifies his identity and deposits a small amount from his bank account (white money). This is necessary for identification and verification purposes and also to later argue that these funds were used as gambling stakes. He then uses his black money to buy some prepaid cards issued by gift card companies. Let's say he purchases 100 such prepaid cards with a value of INR 10,000 each totalling INR 1 Mio. He funds his online gambling account from these prepaid cards.

Darkhorse now gambles in online casino based on a Fixed Odds method as explained above. He plays with INR 1 Million for a period of time. He loses INR 0.95 Mio, wins INR 0.95 Mio and pays gambling fees of INR 0.50 Mio. Money Laundered. And remember, all this is being done is a tax free jurisdiction.

He then instructs the casino to wire the money to his legal bank account. At the same time he calls his bank to give the good news that he has won a jackpot online and expects a wire transfer of INR 9,00,000/- to arrive any time soon.

A layer of complexity is added to the scheme by choosing a casino in an offshore jurisdiction that does not share any information with the financial intelligence of other countries. Darkhorse might have also used the money in his offshore bank account to deposit it in his player account with the casino and then wire transferred the money back to his legal account as lottery winnings.

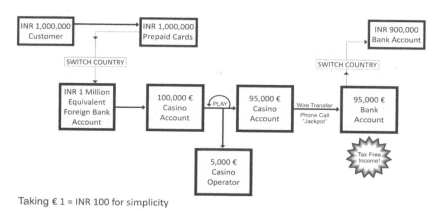

Taking € 1 = INR 100 for simplicity

Modus Operandi 4: Make it large

Mr Darkhorse is so fascinated with online gambling that he decides to launder a big chunk say INR 50 Mio of his drug money by taking advantage of this method.

He chooses a friendly jurisdiction that encourages gambling business and shares no meaningful information with his local FIU governing the AML procedures.

Darkhorse promotes an online casino company, legally owned by him. Some of the best casino gambling software is bought. Recruitments are made and professional experts in the field are hired. Real games are offered to the real customers.

The purpose, however, is not to serve the real customers but conversion of his own black money into white. Accordingly, fake accounts are created (remember we discussed how fake passports are available in our chapter on offshore shell corporations) and games are played in their names. The money in their accounts comes from Darkhorse's anonymous accounts and yes he accepts bitcoins too. The loss of these fictitious players and game fees generates revenues for the casino. His black money gets deposited into his casino's bank account as revenues. Money Laundered.

The net revenues (revenues less expenses) get transferred from the casino's bank account to the bank account of Darkhorse in the country of his choice (Round Tripping). After whole of INR 50 Mio gets laundered this way, the casino shuts its shop.

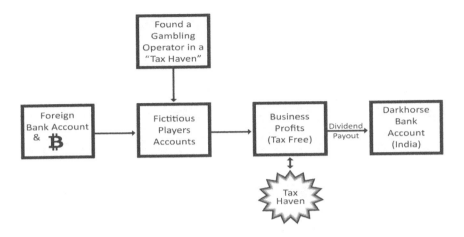

(Tax Haven here refers to a country having Double Tax Avoidance Agreement (DTAA) with India from where Dividends are exempt)

Layers of anonymity and complexity are added in such online gambling houses:

✓ By accepting bitcoins. He can even remit money outwards through bitcoins.

✓ By using browsers like TOR *(as discussed in the chapter on Bitcoins)*

✓ Using Proxy Servers which make a connection appear from a different location than its actual one. Proxy Servers are also used to bypass restrictions that licensed sites have in place to block players from countries where the site owner does not have a proper license.

✓ Use of Virtual Private Network (VPN) which allows anonymity to customers. VPN is a network that is constructed by connecting internet to a private network, such as a company's internal network. VPN uses encryption and other security mechanisms to ensure that data being communicated between the users in the VPN tunnel is not intercepted by any outsider. A number of VPN providers offer their customers the ability to hide their IP addresses and appear to be based in a different city.

Modus Operandi 4: Fixed Odds Betting Terminals (FOBTs):

FOBT is a type of electronic gaming machine over which players bet on the outcome of various simulated games and events (such as roulette, blackjack, bingo, and horse races), the odds offered being fixed from game to game. These machines are installed in shops and are more popular in Europe where the prizes/ jackpot they award can be as high as €500,000 (~ INR 30 Million).

FOBTs involve low transaction amount and high level of anonymity with FOBT shop owners generally keeping minimal record of their customers which can be even fabricated to suit someone's requirements. In many countries, FOBT business remains largely unregulated. A money launderer launders small sums of money through these machines (like Modus Operandi 2 above). Drop by drop, he fills the ocean. And those who wish to launder huge sums of money establish a business of FOB Terminals (like Modus Operandi 4 above).

Players can collect printed tickets from the shops showing they gambled during the particular day and won. Money Laundered.

POINTS TO PONDER:

$ Casinos are similar to Financial Institutions when they undertake activities like accepting remittances on account, maintaining accounts of customers, conducting currency exchange, remitting money to bank accounts etc. Therefore they are required to follow Anti-Money Laundering (AML) procedures and controls.

$ CCTVs are installed on every nook & corner of the casino to record activities of every player on the floor.

$ However, connivance of casino's management and staff leads to money laundering and weak AML compliance.

$ Many tax havens encourage gambling business.

$ Another interesting feature of on-line casino games is directed transfer of money. If Darkhorse wants to pay bribe to Whitehorse who is willing to take the same. Both play an online game – say Poker from their distant locations. Darkhorse will intentionally lose the agreed upon amount to Whitehorse who will claim the amount as Jackpot won and pay applicable taxes thereupon.

$ It is not without logic that in movies, the gangsters and underworld dons are shown as owners of casinos& racing clubs. Gambling involves huge volume of cash transactions which is necessary to obfuscate money laundering transactions.

METHOD 30

Start-Up Companies

Building a successful start-up company has always been a craze. It has now landed in India after its long stint in America and China. Government of India through its Start-up India and Stand-up India programme is also supporting entrepreneurs by providing them funding and relaxing various rules for them. However, behind many genuine start-up companies, there are few who try to cash in from this wave in a wrong way.

Some of the characteristics of start-up companies that make them vulnerable to Money Laundering are:

✓ These companies always need funds for survival through capital or debt and so raising of frequent funds through innovative ways is considered normal.

✓ Even if these companies make continuous losses, their business model is deemed acceptable

✓ Any abrupt increase or decrease in turnover of these companies is considered normal

✓ Their dealings with newly incorporated entities as well as frequent change of trading partners are considered part of their envious negotiation skills.

Let us now look at some of the modi operandi doing rounds with respect to start-ups:

Modus Operandi 1: Raising of Bank Loan fiendishly

1. XYZ Private Limited, a newly established company (Start-up) of Mr Darkhorse desperately needs loan of INR 30 Million from Bank to survive.

2. For sanctioning a loan of INR 30 Mio to XYZ, Bank needs a ballpark turnover of INR 120 Mio whereas the actual turnover of the company is only INR 40 Mio. Thus, a shortfall of INR 80 Mio.

3. Mr Darkhorse, the promoter of XYZ meets Mr Jockey for the purpose and the game begins.

4. Four poor and illiterate people fit for the job are identified. They are Arun (A), Barun (B), Varun (V) and Tarun (T). They are paid good money to sign few documents and a decent regular income is promised to them.

5. Their Income Tax Identification Numbers (PAN in India) are arranged, Income Tax Returns are filed with no tax liability, Bank Accounts are opened, Requisite amount as required for incorporation of companies in their names is deposited in their bank accounts, Director Identification Numbers (DIN) are obtained and other formalities are done.

6. Four new companies are incorporated – Any Private Limited (APL), Many Private Limited (MPL), Give Private Limited (GPL) and Take Private Limited (TPL). All these four companies have their directors from the pool of A, B, V and T. For example: APL has A and B as its promoter directors, MPL has V and T as its promoter directors and likewise these people are promoters in GPL and TPL also. All these companies obtain requisite trade licenses and get ready to do business. *Please note that companies are preferred over partnership firms in Money Laundering schemes so that individuals can hide behind the corporate veil.*

7. Now XYZ books sales of INR 80 Mio over a period of time on APL and MPL and during the same period, it books purchases and expenditures of INR 75 Mio from GPL and TPL. Although these are fictitious transactions but all applicable taxes like VAT/GST and Income Tax are paid on the same. This makes these transactions appear genuine.

   PS: VAT/GST will be levied on difference between Sales and Purchases and Income Tax only on profit, thus not that costly.

8. Based on this bogus additional sales and additional profit of INR 80 Mio and INR 5 Mio (INR 80 Mio – INR 75 Mio) respectively, XYZ is able to raise funds from the Bank as desired.

9. Jockey does a wonderful job in managing the accounts of APL, MPL, GPL and TPL, circulating funds within these companies and filing off their Income Tax Returns.

10. This cycle is repeated many times with many fictitious parties until it becomes too big to hide. In the end, there is a default by XYZ Limited when Darkhorse has successfully siphoned off all the loan funds outside XYZ. Money Laundered through default by a start-up.

Modus Operandi 2: Earning Conversion Income from Black to white

1. XYZ Private Limited, a newly established company (Start-up) of Mr Darkhorse is a stressed company with high leverage (Debt to Equity) ratio of say 4x.

2. Banks and other financiers of XYZ want the company to reduce its leverage which will help it in reducing its interest cost.

3. Darkhorse meets Mr Jockey who agrees to help Darkhorse in reducing his company's leverage.

4. Jockey knows various businessmen who keep scouting for ways to bring in their black money from overseas. One such businessman – Mr Whitehorse is selected by Jockey for the purpose.

5. Whitehorse has an offshore company – WH Inc. in Cyprus controlled through bearer shares that has got INR 10 Mio in Swiss Bank Accounts.

6. Whitehorse needs this money in India in his company - GBPL.

7. Now WH Inc. which is a non-resident invests INR 10 Mio in XYZ Private Limited as Private Equity.

8. XYZ gives outsourcing contracts to GBPL worth INR 10 Mio (less it's agreed upon conversion commission of 5–10%) and later pays this amount to it for fulfilling those contracts.

9. Whitehorse gets his INR 10 Mio in GBPL as desired. Darkhorse gets equity in XYZ; its leverage gets reduced. Financiers are happy with XYZ and its cost of funding is cut down.

10. Darkhorse need not worry about dilution of his equity stake in XYZ because much of the Private Equity amount comes in the form of share premium which is not taxable if it comes from a Non-Resident of India.

Modus Operandi 3: Routing Black Money through other countries into India

1. Suppose Mr Darkhorse has huge amounts of black money stashed in Offshore Banks. He wants to bring the money in India.

2. He incorporates a start-up company with the name XYZ Private Limited and also forms a company overseas.

3. As soon as all the legal formalities relating to registration gets completed, he starts routing the overseas money to the Indian company in small amounts over a period of time.

4. The money so received is disguised as genuine business receipts or overseas investment and kept in the company's bank accounts.

5. Now Darkhorse embezzles the money lying in the company's bank account faking his personal expenses as company expenditure.

6. Darkhorse buys a luxury car, pays himself huge sums as director and even takes his family on an overseas vacation, disguising the expenditure as expenditure incurred on business/ business trips.

7. This process goes on for some time say 2–3 years until the entire money has been siphoned off.

8. Finally, the company XYZ Private Limited is declared as bankrupt. The company will be liquidated and all liabilities will be paid off.

9. Darkhorse' black money may go overseas through Hawala, TBML and come back through various modes be it equity, debt, TBML, P-Notes (equity) etc.

10. Several black money holders, who possess huge amount of undisclosed funds either overseas or in India, look for start-ups to convert their money into white. On the pretext of being an angel investor/ venture capital fund, some of these people take advantage of start-ups and follow the procedure discussed above.

METHOD 31

Tax Amnesty Schemes

"Amnesty is the state's magnanimity to those offenders whom it would be too expensive to punish"

– Ambrose Bierce
(Noted American Journalist)

As stated in my Introduction, tax amnesty schemes are different from other Money Laundering schemes. All other schemes disguise the appearance of black money so that it looks clean (white) whereas amnesty schemes actually convert the black money into white.

In simple language, the government through this scheme demands disclosure of black money and levies tax on such disclosure while promising not to question the source of such black money. In effect, the disclosed black money becomes white.

For example: Mr Darkhorse has lot of black money which he wants to launder. Government comes up with an amnesty scheme with high tax rate of 45%. Darkhorse declares his black money which he wants to launder, and pays 45% tax. Remaining 55% is his white money. No questions asked and money laundered.

Easier said than done, devising such a scheme requires lot of caution. If the tax rate levied is high, people may not be forthcoming with disclosures whereas if the rate is low, it signifies weakness of government to unearth black money on its own. If the schemes are regular, black money holders keep getting benefited and it is a moral hazard for honest people whereas if the schemes are irregular, there is a possibility that large amount of black money accumulated since the last scheme or even prior to that remains undisclosed and untaxed. Further, if the tax rate on amnesty scheme is low, people who foresee their future black money get tempted to launder it in present by disclosing it in advance.

Then, the kind of promise made by government also influences this scheme. If the immunity promised is low i.e. the government does not commit to complete anonymity and/or immunity from prosecution for the crimes behind this money, black money holders may not be forthcoming whereas if the immunity provided is strong, it is akin to cheating with honest citizens of the country and encouraging moral hazard.

Thus, only when tax amnesty schemes are announced and implemented coupled with other black money targeting schemes, they are effective.

POINTS TO PONDER:

$ In India, the tax amnesty schemes have come up since independence. The first one came in 1951 and the last one continues till date.

$ However, this time the government has followed it up with various other Anti-Money Laundering Measures including Demonetisation, searches and seizures, major changes in laws etc.

Thought of Finding Black Money on Street

Not all methods of Money Laundering need to be complex. Some can be as simple as snow but then the effectiveness of such methods is always doubtful.

Here is a method which is overwhelming in its simplicity.

Remember now days, with the advent of demonetisation in India and stringent rules

being framed to prosecute black money holders, people like Darkhorse are willing to convert their black money into white by paying Income Tax applicable over it. Only thing they want is freedom from onerous penalties of 200% to 300% and prosecution proceedings.

Darkhorse who has got a suitcase of full of black money in form of cash and jewellery thinks of using this method.

The modus operandi:

Let me explain this modus operandi by way of a conversation:

Darkhorse enters Income Tax Office with a suitcase full of cash and jewellery.

Income Tax Officer (ITO): Hey, who are you and how dare you bring such a bag into this office.

Darkhorse: Sir, my name is Darkhorse and I want to declare that I while was jogging today morning, I found this suitcase at 3-Lonely Street.

ITO: What? I don't think so? I believe it is your black money stashed in this bag.

Darkhorse: No sir. This belongs to someone else who might have dumped it fearing prosecution since demonetisation and prosecution is going on. I have two witnesses also who saw me jogging today morning and spotting this bag on pavement.

(ITO confused)

Darkhorse: Sir, since I have been lucky to find this bag, I think I should keep it. I am ready to declare it as my income in my Income Tax Return and pay applicable tax on it.

ITO *(still confused)*: OK. Have a seat. Let me discuss the case with my legal associates.

ITO rings up Mr Clean of Clean Law Associates while Darkhorse passes a murky smile.

ITO explains the case to Clean.

Clean: Sir, I don't think we can accept Darkhorse's view even if he has actually found the money in a park or street.

ITO: What is the solution?

Clean: Any person who finds any lost or dumped money or item of someone can keep it only as a Bailee or say caretaker. He is supposed to do all acts that are within his reach to find its real owner and then handover the lost item to him. Accordingly, Darkhorse should have gone to the nearest police station and handed over the bag to police in addition to registering a First Information report (FIR).

ITO: What should I do now?

Clean: You can call the police who will take a note of the situation, seize this bag and file an FIR on its missing owner. The bag should not go back to Darkhorse unless he proves that he is the owner of all this money. He won't do so unless he wants penalty and prosecution.

POINTS TO PONDER:

$ As per the provisions of Indian Contract Act 1872, a person who find goods belonging to another and takes them into his custody, is subject to the same responsibility as a 'Bailee'. He is supposed to take same amount of care of the lost goods as a man of ordinary prudence is expected to take care of his own goods.

$ He is also required to take all necessary actions to find the actual owner of lost goods and all his out of expenses for searching and maintaining the goods will have to be compensated by the owner. It goes without saying that the first action to find the missing owner is to inform police and lodge a FIR.

Conclusion

Change in inevitable. In a progressive country, change is constant"

– Benjamin Disraeli
(Former Prime Minister of the UK)

Since change is only constant, the methods stated in my book are definitely going to change with time. Some are already non-existent and some would be made so but they will always remain here for academic interests of finance enthusiasts. Some new ones may even crop up if we choose not to ignore the ingenuity of Jockeys around the world in this field.

If relevant authorities go through the compilation of methods given here and make necessary changes to curb them one by one, it will ensure that laundering of black money gets eliminated to the maximum extent possible and I will be the happiest person to see these methods getting extinct. Government authorities can also use indirect methods (like change in net worth of the black money holder over a period) and circumstantial evidences to prove concealed income in case no direct evidence is visible.

I feel that curbing black money generation is more important than curbing Money Laundering. If there is no black money, there will be no Money Laundering.

The onus of stopping black money generation falls upon government. I think government needs to check one major thing for this purpose – *Every government official or public servant discharges his/her duty optimally*. If it happens, all the *controllable* black money generation will get controlled. What will remain will be beyond the control of government for which it will have to increase its strength.

Although Prevention of Corruption Act 1988 and other statutory provisions are in place and Government of India is doing its level best to check black money with many think tanks suggesting measures like stringent punishments, stream lining of taxes (where tax rates are lower and compliance is higher), GAAR, GST, forfeitures etc., I too take some liberty to add few suggestions here which are somewhat different:

1. **Education on ill-effects of black money:** Imagine family of a top notch bureaucrat telling him not to do anything that is morally incorrect. Professionals and employees refusing to indulge into malpractices at any cost despite pressure from top. A nation develops when everyone develops and it has to flow from top and not bottom of the pyramid.

2. **Political Governance:** If I have hard earned INR 1000, I will spend it extremely wisely and prudently. Does government also exercises such prudence *in spirit* with respect to public money. If not, taxpayers have got an excuse to lie. If a part of their hard earned money is taken away by government, it should be spent with same responsibility as exercised by the earners (tax payers) of such income. We have stringent corporate governance standards in India that are applied diligently but when it comes to politics, such standards seem missing. The reason for this difference cannot be that corporate entities are more important for our country than political entities or corporates have got more scope for manipulation.

3. **Strengthening judiciary:** Everything should be done to strengthen judiciary so that a strong check and balance system is created and nobody (even government) becomes bigger than law. Autonomy of the judiciary should be maintained to the maximum. Advanced technology, more resources and high quality infrastructure should be provided. More enabling provisions should be there to decide a case based upon circumstantial evidences. Remember, justice delayed is justice denied.

It goes without saying that despite any amount of shortcomings, India is a great country with a huge population of good people and potential around and we should value that.

"We value virtue but do not discuss it. The honest bookkeeper, the faithful wife, the earnest scholar get little of our attention compared to the embezzler, the tramp, the cheat."

John Steinbeck
(American Author)

Here I end my book with this hope that gradually people will move away from Money Laundering and the steps taken by Government of India to curb black money bear fruit.

And so the things will gradually improve…

"*Nai duniya hai, naya daur hai, nayi hai umang.*

Kuch the pehle ke tareeke, to kuch hai aaj ke rang dhang

Roshni aake andheron se jo takrayi hai, kale dhan ko bhi badalna pada aaj apna rang"

(*It's a new world, new era, new aspiration. Some were old ways while some are new. A light has so emerged over darkness that it has forced even the black money to change its colour*)

Arun Jaitley
(Finance Minister, Govt. of India,
while presenting Union Budget 2017)

References

In researching the writings for this book, I have made use of the following print and online sources which shall be beneficial to my readers too:

- $ Money Laundering – A Guide for Criminal Investigators by John Madinger and Sydney A Zalopany
- $ Dirty Dealing by Peter Lilley
- $ Tax Evasion through Shares by Prashant Kumar Thakur
- $ The Panama Papers by Bastian Obermayer and Frederik Obermaier
- $ The Economic Times and www.economictimes.indiatimes.com
- $ Business Standard and www.business-standard.com
- $ HT Mint and www.livemint.com
- $ Business Today and www.businesstoday.in
- $ www.investopedia.com
- $ www.wikipedia.org
- $ www.incometaxindia.gov.in
- $ Financial Action Task Force publications and www.fatf-gafi.org
- $ White paper on Black Money by Ministry of Finance, Government of India
- $ Measures to tackle Black Money in India and Abroad, Report of the committee headed by Chairman, CBDT
- $ Suggestions made by Special Investigation Team (SIT) of India on Black Money

About the Author

Varun Chandna is a Chartered Accountant from India who has worked with some big National and Multinational Banks & Financial Institutions for more than a decade before settling down in his own practice.

His intention of writing this book is to explain Money Laundering to everyone in an interesting manner. In this book, he has also talked about the Great Demonetisation of India, certain tax abuses and the quintessential - Trade Based Money Laundering.